Socrates Meets Jesus

Peter Kreeft

History's Great Questioner Confronts the Claims of Christ

INTERVARSITY PRESS
DOWNERS GROVE, ILLINOIS 60515

For Terry Miethe
and Gary Habermas

InterVarsity Press is the book-publishing division of InterVarsity Christian Fellowship, a student movement active on campus at hundreds of universities, colleges and schools of nursing. For information about local and regional activities, write Public Relations Dept., InterVarsity Christian Fellowship, 6400 Schroeder Rd., P.O. Box 7895, Madison, WI 53707-7895.

Distributed in Canada through InterVarsity Press, 860 Denison St., Unit 3, Markham, Ontario L3R 4H1, Canada.

Cover illustration: Joe DeVelasco

ISBN 0-87784-999-4

Printed in the United States of America

Library of Congress Cataloging in Publication Data

Kreeft, Peter.
  Socrates meets Jesus.

  1. Apologetics—20th century.   I. Title.
BT1102.K73   1987   230   87-13173
ISBN 0-87784-999-4

17	16	15	14	13	12	11	10	9	8	7	6	5	4	3	2	1
99	98	97	96	95	94	93	92	91	90	89	88	87				

CONTENTS

1 From Hemlock to Have It

Socrates, in his usual Greek dress (philosopher's robe), lies completely covered by a sheet on a stone or marble slab of uncertain function in a large basement room in the Broadener Library at Have It University, a renowned hub of learning in Camp Rich, Massachusetts, in the year of Our Lord 1987. The sheet moves. Slowly, tentatively, Socrates lifts a corner and peers out, blinking questioningly.

Socrates: Phaedo! Phaedo! Are you still here? I believe the hemlock is not working as it should. *[Moves his feet, looks at them, then gingerly sits up. Exercises his arms.]* In fact, I feel more alive than ever! *[Throws sheet away.]* Or . . . could it possibly be that I am . . . *[Looks around more eagerly.]* Where am I? Crito? Phaedo? Simmias? Cebes? My friends, my friends! *[Pauses. Looks up.]* Apollo? *[Longer pause. Stock-still. Looks down at his heart.]* Nameless One? *[tremblingly.]*

Flanagan *[barging in with broom]*: Here, now! What's all this fuss and blather? *[Sees Socrates.]* Och! Pardon me, Sir. I dinna know the drama club was rehearsin' here. An' who might ye be, then?

Socrates: Pursuing that question was my lifelong task.

Flanagan: Eh? *Was?* Are ye daft, mon? Think ye to be dead?

Socrates [at a loss, for once]: I . . . I don't really know, to be honest with you. *[Recollects himself.]* I had always believed and taught that the true self was the soul, and that the soul was immortal; therefore I—the true I—am immortal. But I thought my body had just been executed. I drank the entire cup of hemlock. The jailer would not even let me pour out a drop to the gods as a libation. He said they prepared exactly enough.

Flanagan: I'll say this for ye, ye be a good enough actor. Is this dress rehearsal?

Socrates: Hmmm . . . One of the last things I taught my friends before I took the poison was that the true philosopher lives his life as a dress rehearsal for death. "To practice philosophy aright is to practice dying," I said. But I had thought that my opening night had passed. Now I am not so sure. A familiar story—I learn again that my surest surety lies in learning that I am *not* sure. We never seem to learn Lesson One. But . . . what is this place? It does not look like the Isles of the Blest, at least not as I had expected them. But, then, I have learned to distrust all expectations and prejudices, my own first of all, and to welcome surprises, to expect the unexpected. *[Looks through open doorway.]* What's that I see there? Books?

Flannagan: Of course. Five hundred thousand of them here.

Socrates [incredulously]: Five hundred thousand books! Oh . . . perhaps this *is* the Isles of the Blest after all. But where are their authors? I cannot converse with a book. It always gives back the same answer, no matter what you say to it. Surely *some* of their authors reached the Blessed Isles? Is Homer here? I have been looking forward for many years to asking him a few hundred little questions about those gods of his . . .

Flanagan: Ah, I see. Ye still be playin' a part. All right, me friend, I shall play with ye. Have ye some lines for me to read? Or is it ad lib, as they say?

Socrates: Now I am doubly puzzled—that I do not understand your question, and that I *do* understand your barbaric language, though it is not my native Attic tongue and I have never learned it. Perhaps this is *anamnesis*. I had taught that learning is really remembering, but I did not think that included foreign languages, only timeless universal truths. Hmmm . . . *[thinks for ten seconds, shakes his head in puzzlement, turns to Flanagan.]* And you? You do not look like a god, or a blessed spirit. But once again, I must learn to be surprised. What is your name? And more importantly, what is your species?

Flannagan: Me name is Flanagan, and I'm the janitor here. And I'm no god or spirit, unless a red-blooded livin' Scotch-Irishman is a blessed spirit indeed—doubly blessed, I think. But ye're the puzzle, mon, not me. Ye look too old to be a student, unless them makeup people done a masterpiece.

Socrates: Oh, no. Never too old to be a student.

Flanagan: Are ye enrolled here, then?

Socrates: Here? Where is here, please?

Flanagan: Why, Have It, of course.

Socrates: Have what? What are you offering me?

Flanagan: No, Have It University here in Camp Rich, Massachusetts. The heart of academia.

Socrates: Academia! My disciple Plato had grandiose plans for a thing he called his "academy," in the grove of Academe. Has it indeed come to this? This . . . ? *[Gestures.]*

Flanagan: Ye might say so, yes.

Socrates: What goes on here? Is this the heart of the Ideal State?

Flanagan: Nah! It's just the Broadener Library. What's supposed to go on here is that all these books are supposed to broaden yer mind. Though I always says, about all this learnin' does to people is to make little crazies into big ones. But do ye really not know where ye are? Do ye have amnesia?

Socrates: Only in the same sense we all have it, I think: forgetfulness indeed, forgetfulness of who we really are.

Flannagan: Ah, I see. You belong here, all right, right among the crazies. A philosopher, right?

Socrates: That is what I am, yes. A lover of wisdom.

Flannagan: Ye are just playin' a part, now, are ye not?

Socrates: I assure you, I am quite serious. The last thing I remember before waking up in this place was drinking the poison and waiting for death to take me. You are not Death, are you?

Flannagan: Is Death a janitor?

Socrates: Many of my people thought he was a ferryman.

Flannagan: But now what did ye go and drink poison for?

Socrates: Oh, it wasn't suicide, I assure you. I was executed.

Flanagan: Executed, now! An' by whom, pray tell?

Socrates: By the five hundred plus one, of course. The jailer's hand that gave me the cup was no more bloody than my own. Both were commanded by the will of the people. Those silly democrats believed that "the voice of the people is the voice of God." I certainly hope you've gotten over *that* superstition here, wherever here is.

Flanagan: I just told ye where here is. An' don't go knockin' the Democrats. Yer clothes don't look rich enough for ye to be a Republican.

Socrates: I don't understand. This place is not my prison cell, and you are not an Athenian. Was I spirited away into exile at the last minute by my friends? I pleaded with Crito not to do that. What foreign land is Cabbage, Massachusetts?

Flanagan: If ye are really serious, ye must have had a bad dream and ye woke up with amnesia.

Socrates [puzzled, thoughtful]: I often thought of comparing life to a dream, because death always seemed to be an awakening. But life always seemed more real to me than any dream. And so does this.

Flanagan: Do ye know yer name, at least?

Socrates: Of course. My name is Socrates.

Flanagan: Why, sure it is. And mine is Einstein.

Socrates: I don't understand. I thought you told me your name was Flanagan.

Flanagan [aside]: By gum, I think the little fellow's really daft! *[to Socrates.]* Look here, let's try to get ye settled somehow. Have ye got any identification on ye?

Socrates: My face was identification enough for anyone in Athens.

Flanagan: Ho! I can see why. Mon, that's one froggy face for ye!

Socrates: So people say. And I thought I had croaked, as they say. But now . . . *[Fumbles in robe, pulls out pink registration slip.]* I seem to have a piece of paper with me. Colored paper! How strange. Like a rose. What does this mean? *[Reads, shakes head, hands to Flanagan.]* Can you interpret this for me? I understand the words but not the meaning. They all seem to be nouns. I can't find any sentences. What a strange barbaric grammar! How can one noun modify another noun?

Flanagan: Let's see. *[Scowls, reads, relaxes.]* Oh. "Have It Divinity School." Aye, that's the Div School. And this is your registration form. By gum, it even has yer name on it. It has ye registered under the name of Socrates. I guess the computer has a sense of humor. In any case, ye are a student at the Have It Divinity School.

Socrates: Divinity School? Then this is heaven? Am I to learn how to become divine?

Flanagan: Are ye tryin' to funny me, mon?

Socrates: No, Einstein, I am not.

Flanagan: Now cut that out. Dinna call me Einstein!

Socrates: As you please, Flanagan. Are you the janitor of the gods?

Flanagan: By God, ye are daft as a daisy!

Socrates: You swear by God rather than by the gods! Few knew that great secret in my city. This must be the Isles of the Blest indeed!

Flanagan: Oh, come off it, mon. Nobody talks about the gods nowadays.

Socrates: Have I been moved in time as well as place?

Flanagan: Well, if ye are Socrates, I'll say ye have. A couple of thousand years, at least, I reckon. *[Sudden thought.]* Hey? Is there black magic goin' on here? I'll have nought to do with divil's work! If ye're lyin', I'll play with ye, an' if ye're sick I'll help ye, but if ye're playin' with black magic, ye're too sick for me to help ye.

Socrates: As I told you, Flanagan, I have no idea how I got here. But it feels too good to be the work of black magic, and it doesn't feel good enough to be heaven. Though I distrust feeling, I have nothing else to go by so far, so until further evidence is in, I shall conclude that I am probably still on earth.

Flanagan: Why, of course ye are, mon! Feel yer bones, now. That's no spirit, fer sure.

Socrates: The important question, though, is not *where* I am—the material—but *why* I am—the spiritual, the design. Have you any idea why I was put here?

Flanagan: Not a clue. Unless ye are here to help me clean this pig pen. Those kids throw their trash wherever they've a mind to, and this old janitor has to clean up two days' trash every single day. But I suppose ye have other things to do. Like the Divinity School.

Socrates: Yes, that seems to be the place for me. I am a lifelong student, for one thing, and for another, this registration paper seems to be a sign for me to follow. I have always believed that all things, even the strangest, are governed by a perfect divine plan, and that no evil can possibly happen to a good man, whether in this life or in the next. So I shall take the adventure sent me by God, whatever it be. *[Prepares to walk away. Looks at his clothes, then Flanagan's.]* I suppose I shall look rather out of place if everyone here dresses like you?

Flanagan: Oh, don't worry. There's no law against togas. They have everything there, Moonies, Libbies, gays, even fundamentalists.

Socrates: Some time I shall have to explore these strange creatures. There are just so many questions I want to ask . . .
Flanagan: Say, there, a piece of advice to ye, if ye don't mind? Now
ye don't want to ask too many questions, or the wrong kind, if
ye want to stay outa trouble.
Socrates: Alas, that warning has an all-too-familiar sound! *[Pause.]*
Now I know I am not in heaven. For as I said in my last speech,
I don't suppose philosophers get in trouble *there* for asking ques-
tions, as I did in Athens. Hmmm. Seems we have another Athens
here. So the Divinity School is not a school for apprentice gods,
then?
Flanagan: O, ho, that's a good one. I think some of the characters
there act like they thought they was apprentice gods, all right.
An' maybe not even apprentices.
Socrates: I think I must have been sent here for the same reason
I was sent to Athens, and by the same God: to help people remember who they really are.
Flanagan: Look here, I wish I could come with ye. I foresee a pack
o' trouble ahead for the likes of ye, an' let no one laugh at an old
Irishman's prophecies. But my job is to clean up the mess here,
and yers seems to be to clean up another kind of mess, or to try,
anyways . . . somethin' like that. I'm not sure just what I mean.
When the fit is on the prophet, he goes a step out of his mind,
don't ye know.
Socrates: I think I know, friend, and I thank you for the friendly
advice. I think I should like to check back with you, if you don't
mind, after I try the adventure over there in the Divinity School.
You seem to be ballast for my journey, an anchor in earth and
common sense as I venture on the seas and airs of philosophy.
May we converse again later?
Flanagan: Why, sure, mon, that's in the cards, I think. Go now.
I'll be around when ye need me. I'm always wanderin' around this
place to and fro. Sometimes ye see me and sometimes ye don't.
Socrates: Thank you, Flanagan. God be with you. *[Exits.]*

Flanagan: Oh, he is, he is. *[Looking toward the door at the departing Socrates.]* Now what the divil did they mean sendin' him here, I wonder?

2 Progressing Away from Progress

Socrates stands on a street corner in Have It Square in Camp Rich, Massachusetts, looking quite square. He gazes at the traffic, both vehicular and human, with something between amusement and amazement, looking first fascinated, then thoughtful, then compassionate; first puzzled, then pondering, then pitying. These three moods take some time to cross the wide seas of his face, like tides. As the third tide turns, Bertha Broadmind, a student at Have It Divinity School, spots him and rivets her attention on him. She too is first puzzled, then pondering, then pitying. As Socrates begins to drift away in no particular direction, looking in vain for a familiar point of reference, Bertha rushes up to him.

Bertha: Socrates! Is it really you?

Socrates [surprised and pleased]: Why, yes. How do you know me? Were you sent here to meet me? I expected a messenger of the gods, but forgive me, you do not look the part.

Bertha: Oh, Socrates! You're so—so Socratic! It *is* you, isn't it?

Socrates: Of course I am I, unless the law of noncontradiction has been abolished here. But where is *here?*

Bertha: Socrates, you are in the hub of academia, the brain center of the world, Have It University. This is what your disciple Plato's great invention came to. This is where we train many of our philosopher-kings, or the closest thing. In fact— let's see—that card you're holding looks like a registration card for Have It Divinity School. Yes, it is! Why, you're going to be in some of my classes. Fantastic! Come on, I'll help you find your way around registration.

Socrates: It seems I must be led by you. As we go, could you explain some of the strange sights these old eyes of mine are seeing? There seem to be no holding places in my mind for them.

Bertha: I'd love to, Socrates. What a privilege for *me* to teach *you!*— about all the progress the world has made since your day. How wonderful it must be for you to see over two thousand years of progress in one day!

Socrates [stopping short in the middle of the street]: Did you say *two thousand years?*

Bertha [jerking him back]: Watch your step, Socrates! Taxis don't stop for philosophers here.

Socrates: Flanagan? Now that is very strange. I thought I saw . . . Never mind. That—that thing was a "taxi"?

Bertha: People don't walk long distances anymore. They ride in cars. Yes, all those things are cars. Would you like a ride in one?

Socrates: I think I'd prefer to walk.

Bertha: Are you afraid?

Socrates: No, I enjoy walking. Don't people enjoy walking any more? Those *car* things seem to be a way to *avoid* walking, aren't they?

Bertha: I guess you could look at it that way.

Socrates: I don't understand why you would prefer to sit inside one of those mechanical animals rather than using your own two good legs out in the open air.

Bertha: Why, they get you where you're going much faster, of course.

Socrates: Of course, but why would you want to shorten one of life's great little pleasures, walking?

Bertha: I never thought of that.

Socrates: I begin to see why I was sent here. I don't claim to understand your world, but it seems to me that the noise and hubbub and danger of those things would make travel decidedly unpleasant. Do the people inside them who guide them *enjoy* being in them?

Bertha: Not usually. Not now, at rush hour, anyway.

Socrates: That's what I thought. I noticed most of the drivers look rather glum or impatient. I suppose they are impatient to end their unpleasant journey in this vehicle?

Bertha: Yes.

Socrates: In that case, why do they choose to travel in cars in the first place? Why not walk if walking is more pleasant? They seem to be locking themselves into unpleasant little cages and going as fast as possible so that they can get out of their cages as fast as they can. Why get in in the first place?

Bertha: They have to get where they're going in a hurry. To work, for instance.

Socrates: But why would they want to rush to work? Why not take a pleasant, leisurely walk to work instead?

Bertha: They don't have the time to walk to work.

Socrates: Why not?

Bertha: Most of them live far from their work.

Socrates: Why?

Bertha: There isn't enough room to have houses where the offices are, I guess . . . I don't know.

Socrates: Those buildings are offices?

Bertha: Some, yes.

Socrates: And do people enjoy working in them?

Bertha: Not usually. But there are all sorts of jobs, of course . . .

Socrates: Do most people enjoy their jobs here?

Bertha: Some do and some don't, I guess. I don't know how you could know that for sure.

Socrates: Perhaps asking a question would help: If they were given free room and board by the State for the rest of their lives and didn't have to do any work for it, would they then do the work they do now if they didn't get paid anything extra for it?

Bertha: Most people wouldn't.

Socrates: Then they do not work for the work but for the pay.

Bertha: Yes.

Socrates: Are they all slaves then?

Bertha: Oh, no. We have no slaves, Socrates. That's one of the best pieces of progress we ever made since your day. We don't need slaves anymore. We have machines to do our work for us.

Socrates: Then why not send the machines to work in those cars and offices instead of the people who don't enjoy it?

Bertha: In a way, we do. But we have to monitor the machines.

Socrates: Then you are slaves to your slaves?

Bertha: Certainly not. We are all free.

Socrates: Then why is work such a drudgery for free men?

Bertha: Women too, Socrates. We're not male chauvinists any more. That's another piece of progress—equality among the sexes.

Socrates: You mean women work too?

Bertha: Usually.

Socrates: So your women are just as enslaved as your men?

Bertha: Enslaved?

Socrates: Enslaved to the need to work at unpleasant jobs just for the sake of money.

Bertha: Socrates, try not to be so critical.

Socrates: You mean try not to be myself? A difficult task.

Bertha: I mean, try to look at it from our point of view.

Socrates: I'm trying, but I am not succeeding. I don't understand why the faces of most of the people I see are so unhappy, if you have made such progress. Why is everyone hurrying nervously about like slaves worried about displeasing their masters?

Bertha: It's not as bad as that, Socrates.

Socrates: Let us see. *[He stops a group of very assorted people.]* Excuse me, good people, but would any of you have a free hour or two to converse with me about the best things in life, about virtue and truth?

Passerby 1: You gotta be kidding!

Passerby 2: Who's that weirdo?

Passerby 3: Virtue and truth! Is that a brand of pot?

Socrates: You see, Bertha? That is what I do not understand.

Bertha: They just don't have the time, Socrates.

Socrates: But if your machines give you leisure, who steals it from you?

Bertha: No one.

Socrates: Then you give it away freely? This is even more astonishing!

Bertha [pulling Socrates back onto the curb just in time]: Look out for the red light! You know, you really must concentrate more on where you're going instead of all this head-in-the-clouds talk about virtue and truth, you know.

Socrates: Did *you* just save my life? I seem to see . . . Well, thank you. So even your walks are dangerous here. But you seem to have avoided the most dangerous thing of all.

Bertha: What's that?

Socrates: Philosophy.

Bertha: Oh, we have philosophers here.

Socrates: Where are they?

Bertha: In the philosophy department.

Socrates: Philosophy is not department.

Bertha: Well, we have philosophers.

Socrates: Are they dangerous?

Bertha: Of course not.

Socrates: Then they are not true philosophers. Tell me does no one in your world obey the god's first commandment?

Bertha: What's that?

Socrates: Know thyself.

Bertha: Oh, sure. Plenty of people go to psychiatrists and psychologists . . .

Socrates: Are they philosophers?

Bertha: They're like doctors for the soul. People go to them to get rid of their troubles.

Socrates: Then they are not philosophers. Philosophers *make* troubles.

Bertha: You *would* say that, Socrates. But no one gets executed for philosophizing today.

Socrates: Is that because they care about philosophy? Or because they do *not* care?

Bertha: I guess most don't care. They're bored with philosophy.

Socrates: Now there is a word I do not understand. What is it to be "bored"?

Bertha: I don't get it. You speak perfect English. Why don't you understand that word?

Socrates: English . . . yes. Somehow, I find myself speaking your barbaric language without ever having learned it. Yet I have not forgotten my own. And here is a word that has no equivalent in my language. Perhaps people started getting what you called "bored" only in your time. Might it be connected with the worship of your new god?

Bertha: God?

Socrates: Progress.

Bertha: Progress is not a god, Socrates.

Socrates: If you know that, then why do you treat it as a god?

Bertha: Do you think we do that? Most of us believe in only one God, just as you did.

Socrates: Aha! So my secret is known, after all these years? Then tell me something else: How do you find your silence and solitude in this world so you can commune with your God and with yourself and your thoughts?

Bertha: Come to think of it, we don't have much silence or solitude in our world.

Socrates: So it seems. Why not?

Bertha: I guess we don't like it very much. In fact, come to think of it, that's what we give to our most desperate criminals as a punishment, the worst punishment we conceive.

Socrates: You're not serious? The great gift of solitude? The thing the sages long for as a gift more precious than gold?

Bertha: I'm afraid that's the way it is, Socrates.

Socrates: I begin to see why I was sent here. But I do not see why you call all this "progress." Is your whole world as ugly as this place?

Bertha: Quiet, Socrates! You'll insult the natives. This place is Have It Square, and it's one of the most popular places to live. People pay twice as much to live here as out in the country.

Socrates: Oh, then, you do still have open country, then.

Bertha: Yes.

Socrates: Where there is green grass, and healthy trees, and air that smells like air?

Bertha: Yes. There's plenty of unspoiled open country.

Socrates: But if you prefer to live in places like this, why do you call your countryside "unspoiled"? Why do you prefer to live in places you call "spoiled"?

Bertha: I don't know. I guess because we find the country boring.

Socrates [with a sigh]: There's that word again! An invention of yours that I think we did not know.

Bertha: Didn't anyone get bored in your Athens, Socrates?

Socrates: I suppose not, for if they had, they would have invented a word for it. We Greeks were very good at that, you know, inventing words.

Bertha: But you lived in the city instead of the country, didn't you?

Socrates: But Athens was a beautiful city. *[Another sigh.]* I suppose it's all gone now?

Bertha: No, the ruins are still stand. It's a very popular tourist spot. Even the Parthenon is still standing, most of it.

Socrates: Oh! I should dearly love to visit it. How far away is it? Could we walk there?

Bertha [laughing]: No, Socrates, it's thousands of miles away across the ocean. You have to fly there.

Socrates: I think you mistake my identity. The name is Socrates, not Icarus.

Bertha [laughing more]: No, I mean in a plane. A mechanical bird. It flies at a thousand miles an hour.

Socrates: How like a god! *[Thoughtfully]*—and how unlike! But tell me, why do tourists still visit the ruins of old Athens?

Bertha: Why, because it was so beautiful, of course.

Socrates: I don't understand, then. If you admit that Athens is more beautiful than Camp Rich, Massachusetts, then why don't you build cities like Athens instead of cities like Camp Rich? Have you forgotten the knowledge or lost the skill?

Bertha: No.

Socrates: Then why not?

Bertha: Because you just can't turn back the clock, Socrates.

Socrates: Of course you can. And should, if it keeps bad time. As it seems your world is keeping.

Bertha: That's very clever, Socrates.

Socrates: No, it is not clever. It is simple and serious. Why not? It was not a rhetorical question; it was a plea for an answer.

Bertha: Because you can't turn back progress, of course.

Socrates: Oh, yes, I had forgotten. Your juggernaut god is very demanding and very jealous.

Bertha: Progress is not a god. It serves us, we don't serve it.

Socrates: Is that so? Then has it made you happier?

Bertha: I . . . I guess I don't know.

Socrates: Do you think it should?

Bertha: I guess so.

Socrates: Let's see whether we can improve your knowledge from a guess to a certainty by finding a proof. If a master is served by a slave, does the master expect to be made happier in some way by this service?

Bertha: Of course. Otherwise he wouldn't have a slave.

Socrates: And Progress, you say, is your slave rather than your master?

Bertha: Yes.

Socrates: Then you must expect it to make you happier.

Bertha: That follows.

Socrates: The next thing to ask, then, is whether it has done that for you. Are people in your day happier than they were before Progress came?

Bertha: I don't know.

Socrates: If you don't know whether it has made you happier or not, then why do you choose it?

Bertha: I guess it does make us happier today. But I don't know how you can tell that. How can you compare two different cultures?

Socrates: By looking for clues. There seem to be many. For instance, is there less discontent expressed in your literature? Less political unrest and revolution, less restless change in the world? Fewer and smaller wars, fewer people changing their lives, their jobs, their homes, their wives or husbands out of discontent? Less mental disorder? Fewer crimes? Fewer rapes, child abuse, infanticide, abortion? Less fear of death for the individual and for the society? Less uncertainty about whether life is worth living?

Bertha [sighing]: No, Socrates, there's more.

Socrates: More of what?

Bertha: More of all those things.

Socrates [incredulous]: More of *all* of those things?

Bertha: Yes.

Socrates [still unbelieving]: Every one?

Bertha: Yes.

Socrates: One thing, then, at least, seems abundantly clear: people in your society are much less happy than people in mine.

Bertha: I guess I have to admit that.

Socrates: And you nevertheless still believe in Progress?

Bertha: Of course I do.

Socrates: What strong faith you have in your god!

Bertha: It's not *faith*, Socrates.

Socrates: Well, it's certainly not reason and evidence.

Bertha: I'm all confused. Look, here we are at Divinity Avenue. There's Divinity Hall down there.

Socrates: It doesn't look very divine. Is that the Divinity School?

Bertha: No, the Div is on Francis Avenue.

Socrates: Can we go to it that way, down Divinity Avenue? Perhaps we will meet a few gods?

Bertha: No, Divinity Ave is a dead end.

Socrates: I could have told you that.

Bertha: What?

Socrates: I mean that the ambition to turn into a god is not very promising.

Bertha: My only ambition right now is to turn into a street.

Socrates: But I think you are trying to turn into a god—your new god Progress. It seems you have become just like your god, ever moving, never thinking. Ah, there's a bench. Do you mind if we act contrary to the nature of your god for just a moment? I mean if we both stop and think? Let's just sit here and finish our conversation before we tackle another piece of Progress called "registration."

Bertha: All right. I'd like to get to the bottom of this progress thing.

Socrates: Good for you. Now that's what I call progress.

Bertha: You said progress is our master, not our slave. But that can't be. We're the masters of the universe. We've conquered nature. That's what progress means. You can't deny that, at least.

Socrates: Perhaps not, but shall we inquire?

Bertha: Certainly.

Socrates: You say you control nature now?

Bertha: Yes. Much more than in the past, anyway.

Socrates: Tell me, what would you say of this case. Imagine a chariot drawn by four headstrong horses. I suppose you could just as well use one of those *car* things of yours as an example. Now imagine a small child at the reins. At the child's slightest touch the horses obey. The child controls the horses, and the horses control the chariot. But what controls the child? Suppose the child is as blind and as headstrong as the horses. Suppose he does not control himself, does not control his own control. Would you say then that he is in control of the chariot?

Bertha: Are you saying that's an image of our world?

Socrates: I'm asking. *Do* you control your control? Are you a people with great self-control?

Bertha: No. I think we're a very violent people.

Socrates: Then the chariot of your society is in danger.

Bertha: You don't know the half of it, Socrates. At this very moment two rival nations have weapons called thermonuclear bombs that can destroy every single living thing on earth, and they fundamentally mistrust each other.

Socrates: By Zeus! A wayward child with a giant's weapon! What a dangerous combination!

Bertha: And I think we're worried about our control too because one of our most popular stories is about a Doctor Frankenstein who creates a mechanical monster who runs amok.

Socrates: Oh, I do not see your machines running amok. It seems you are controlling them fairly well. But you seen to be worried about yourselves—for instance, about whether you will be foolish enough to use those terrible weapons.

Bertha: I don't think we're that foolish, Socrates.

Socrates: Then why don't you just get rid of all those weapons? Then both sides will breathe a sigh of relief and be happier.

Bertha: Maybe we *are* that foolish, Socrates. What you say is perfectly reasonable, but we don't do it.

Socrates: And even if you are *not* so foolish as to use your weapons, your machines do not seem to be making you happy. So they do not seem to be working as your slaves. And so they are a poor proof of progress, and of power.

Bertha: They've made us wiser, anyway. We know much more than you old Greeks did.

Socrates: Do you mean that knowledge alone makes you wise? Is knowledge the same as wisdom?

Bertha: No, but we have more knowledge, at least.

Socrates: Which is more valuable, knowledge or wisdom?

Bertha: Wisdom.

Socrates: Then where is your modern wisdom?

Bertha: Actually, we usually speak of "ancient wisdom" and "modern knowledge" rather than the reverse.

Socrates: So you admit that the ancients were wiser while you moderns have more knowledge.

Bertha: I guess so.

Socrates: And you know that wisdom is more valuable?

Bertha: Yes.

Socrates: Then why have you exchanged the more valuable thing for the less? And why do you call this "progress"?

Bertha: Well, at least we know more. We've made progress in that area anyway.

Socrates: Do you know things like birth and death and love and hate and life and God more than we did?

Bertha: Certainly. We know thousands of things about them that you never knew.

Socrates: You may know more *about* them, but do you know *them* more?

Bertha: I don't see the distinction you're making.

Socrates: You know, for instance, what the weather is going to be tomorrow much more accurately than we did, I suspect.

Bertha: Yes.

Socrates: But do you think you know the weather itself better than a sailor or a farmer who has lived with it as his constant companion all his life?

Bertha: Oh, I see. Well, in a way no, but in another way yes. We can control it better. Because of our knowledge we can control many forces in nature that you never dreamed of controlling. We can fly to the moon, for instance . . .

Socrates: Remarkable indeed! And is it a delightful place to live?

Bertha: No, there's no life there. You can't live there.

Socrates: Then why is it so good to go there?

Bertha: Must you question everything?

Socrates: Yes.

Bertha: Look, take something else. We can communicate with someone ten thousand miles away instantly, faster than the messenger of the gods. Surely that's progress.

Socrates: It is, if you have something worthwhile to say.

Bertha: We can grow food ten times more efficiently.

Socrates: And so you have abolished starvation?

Bertha: Well, no . . . But we can cure thousands of diseases.

Socrates: I didn't know there *were* thousands of diseases. Have you invented some new ones?

Bertha: I—I just can't believe I'm hearing this from you, Socrates. I always thought you were a progressive.

Socrates: What is a progressive?

Bertha: One who is ahead of his time.

Socrates: How can someone be ahead of his time? Can you travel into the future faster than time does?

Bertha: It means ahead of other people in your time. For instance, didn't you stand up for freedom of speech and the rights of man and the sacredness of every man's opinion in your Apology, your last speech before the court that condemned you to death?

Socrates: If Plato reported my speech correctly, you will find none of those ideas there. Perhaps you misread it.

Bertha: What? Do you deny those ideas?

Socrates: I did not say that. Shall we investigate them?

Bertha: No, not now. There's no time.

Socrates: In my day, there would have been time. But you live amid so much progress . . .

Bertha: What *do* you believe in, Socrates, if you don't believe in those things or in progress?

Socrates: As I said at my trial, I believe in the god, though I cannot name him.

Bertha: But a god is unchanging, isn't it?

Socrates: Yes. That was one of the reasons I did not name the god Zeus or even Apollo. The gods my fellow Athenians believed in were as changeable as the wind, or one of those traffic lights of yours.

Bertha: But if your god is unchanging, you live in a static world. There's no possibility of progress.

Socrates: Exactly the opposite, I think.

Bertha: What?

Socrates: Only if the god does not progress, can we progress.

Bertha: How do you figure that?

Socrates: Would you not define progress as change for the better?

Bertha: Yes.

Socrates: And "better" means "closer to the best"?

Bertha: Yes.

Socrates: And the god is the best?

Bertha: Yes.

Socrates: Good. I too believe that. My countrymen believed in gods who were something less than the best. Well, then, if progress means change toward the best, and if the god *is* the best, then progress means change toward the god.

Bertha: So?

Socrates: The god, then, is the goal of progress.

Bertha: I still don't see what the point of all this is.

Socrates: Suppose the god, the goal of progress, is changing. Then progress becomes impossible. How could we progress toward a goal that keeps receding? How could a runner make progress toward a finish line if someone kept moving it as he ran?

Bertha: He couldn't.

Socrates: Then if the god progresses, you cannot progress, for the god is your goal. Without an unchanging goal you cannot judge any change as progress. So you can have no hope.

Bertha: Of course we have hope.

Socrates: What is your hope?

Bertha: A better world.

Socrates: But what *is* a better world? How can you know what world is better without the best as a standard?

Bertha: We just live in hope.

Socrates: Without defining its object?

Bertha: Yes, without defining its object. That would limit it. Arriving at an end would be boring. It's the getting there that's good. "It is better to travel hopefully than to arrive."

Socrates: Oh, no. That, at least, cannot be.

Bertha: Why not?

Socrates: If you do not hope to arrive, then how can you travel hopefully? There is nothing to hope *for*.

Bertha: More hope is what we hope for. One of our wise men said, "There's nothing to fear but fear itself." Hope is like that too. There's nothing to hope for but hope itself.

Socrates: But how can you hope in hope itself? Hope in hope? Hope in what? I suppose you are also in love with love rather than being in love with anyone? Do you have faith in faith rather than faith in the god?

Bertha: What's wrong with that?

Socrates: That is like a hall of mirrors, with nothing outside them to appear in them. Like Narcissus, you see only your own reflection.

Bertha: Socrates, I'm really disappointed in you. I thought you'd be more up to date than this.

Socrates: Up to date?

Bertha: This is 1987.

Socrates: And I am here. So I am quite up to date.

Bertha: But you don't *believe* in 1987.

Socrates: Of course not. How can one believe in a number?

Bertha: I mean you don't believe in progress.

Socrates: I have been trying to tell you that for a long time now, and making little progress. No, I don't. I did not believe in the fashionable and up-to-date gods my countrymen believed in either, and I got myself executed for that. Tell me, do people still believe in Zeus today?

Bertha: No. No one.

Socrates: Well, then, don't you see? The beliefs that were most up to date in my world were the ones that were soon dated. And the same thing will happen to yours, I assure you, including this new god Progress. And when that happens, that will be real progress.

Bertha: Oh, look. Here we are at the Div. There's the registration line. Listen, I have to register myself on the second floor. Do you think you can stay out of trouble for a few minutes? I suppose not. Look. Here's a newspaper. Why don't you read it as you're waiting in line? It will give you some idea of what's going on in our world.

Socrates: The New Yuck *Times?*

Bertha: Yes, that's the name of our greatest newspaper.

Socrates: I prefer to read the eternities. I don't suppose you have such a publication here?

Bertha: We like to keep up with the times here at the Divinity School.

Socrates: I suppose it was too much to expect, but I did hope that a "divinity school" would have something to do with the eternities. Are none of your gods eternal?

Bertha: That's one of the things we argue about here.

Socrates [brightening]: Do you really? Then perhaps this is the right place for me after all.

3 Was Jesus a Fundamentalist?

Bertha Broadmind finds Socrates milling around during registration at the Have It Divinity School. Socrates looks rather lost, so Bertha works her way through the crowd to his side.

Bertha: Are you finished registering, Socrates?

Socrates: I think so. My pink card already had my courses listed on it, so I concluded that whoever arranged for me to be here also arranged for my courses. I still have no idea who that was. Presumably only a god could move people about in time like that, so I had better follow his leading, whoever he is. Perhaps I was sent here to find out. Or to find out who I am. Or both. Somehow those two questions seem inextricably intertwined.

Bertha: Let's see what courses you're in, Socrates. Hmmm. Science and Religion, Comparative Religions, Fundamentals of Demythologizing . . . Oh, good! I'll be in some of your courses with you.

Socrates: What in the world is "demythologizing"?

Bertha: It's a way out of fundamentalism. Fundamentals of Demythologizing means demythologizing fundamentalism.

Socrates: But what is fundamentalism?

Bertha: Fundamentalism is basically narrow-minded thinking, forcing everything into rigid, preconceived little categories.

Socrates: Is one of these thinking machines of yours—computers—is a computer a fundamentalist, then?

Bertha: Oh. I guess I'll have to narrow my definition a bit.

Socrates: Then would that narrow thinking make you a fundamentalist?

Bertha: I don't know whether to take you seriously or not. No, fundamentalism doesn't mean just any narrow thinking. It's a religious term. A fundamentalist forces everything and everybody into his narrow little religious categories.

Socrates: What categories are those?

Bertha: Basically, the saved and the damned. They say if you're not born again like them, you're going to hell.

Socrates: And this idea—whatever it means—is repellent to you, I take it.

Bertha: It certainly is. It's a most un-Christian attitude.

Socrates: What is a Christian? I take it you are one?

Bertha: I'm taking religious studies here.

Socrates: That was not my question.

Bertha: I might even seek to be ordained as a minister.

Socrates: You still have not answered my question.

Bertha: Oh. Well, I just can't believe that if you're not born again, you're going to hell.

Socrates: I guess you're not going to answer my question. Well, let's try another. I presume you have reasons for what you do and do not believe?

Bertha: Of course.

Socrates: Well?

Bertha: What do you mean, well? Oh. I see. You want to know *why* I don't believe in fundamentalism. Why, because it's damned narrow.

Socrates: I thought you said they thought they were the saved, and their way was too narrow. So they would be "saved narrow," not "damned narrow," wouldn't they?

Bertha: Huh?

Socrates: Please just tell me why you believe fundamentalism is not true.

Bertha: Oh. Well, because if it were, then most of the world would be going to hell, and only a small, select elite would make it to heaven.

Socrates: Oh. How do you know that?

Bertha: Why, because it logically follows, of course. Don't you see that?

Socrates: I might, if I look. Let's look. From what premises does that conclusion follow?

Bertha: It's so simple, Socrates. If only the born again are saved, and only a few are born again, then only a few are saved. Didn't you ever take logic?

Socrates: Take it? I gave it to the world.

Bertha: Oh. Sorry. I forgot.

Socrates: But let us look at your syllogism, if you don't mind. It certainly seems impeccable, but I would like to peck at the impeccable, if possible. Your argument is really a *reductio ad absurdum*, as your language calls it. You deny the fundamentalist premise that only the born again are saved because it logically entails the absurd conclusion that only a few are saved. Isn't that correct?

Bertha: Yes.

Socrates: Then my question is, How do you know the conclusion is absurd?

Bertha: Don't you think it is?

Socrates: What *I* think is not what we are investigating now, but what *you* think. I do not know anything about this strange new beast called fundamentalism, but you do. You are teaching me, remember? So now please do this service for me, and continue to teach me.

Bertha: What do you want to know?

Socrates: What I already asked twice and was not answered—How do you know that the conclusion that only a few are saved is false?

Bertha: I just can't believe it, that's all. It's absurd.

Socrates: You have no reason for this belief of yours?

Bertha: Must I give a reason for everything I believe?

Socrates: If you agree that the unexamined life is not worth living, then you must indeed. You must be prepared to give a reason for the faith that is in you.

Bertha: Aha! You just blew your cover, "Socrates." Where did you pick up that quotation?

Socrates: The unexamined life? Why, I invented it. Thousands of years ago. In my swan song, the *Apology.* I know it's still around because I just saw a copy of it on that bookshelf over there. What do you mean, I "blew my cover"?

Bertha: I meant the other quotation, about giving a reason. That's from the Bible. When did you read the Bible?

Socrates: I didn't. And that was no quotation. I just said it because I thought it to be true.

Bertha: You mean you say exactly the same thing as St. Paul?

Socrates: I don't know who he is, but would that be so surprising, if truth were the same in two different mouths?

Bertha: You're almost as clever as he was, I'll say that for you. Look, if you're all finished registering, maybe we should just call it a day. I'll see you in class.

Socrates: I don't understand. How can you not want to finish the investigation? We just began. It's like hearing half a song. Won't you stay and sing the other half to me, for my sake if not for yours? I still have no idea what this awful beast fundamentalism really is.

Bertha: Oh, all right. Where were we?

Socrates: The argument was that fundamentalism must be false because it says that only the born again are saved, and only a few are born again, therefore only a few would be saved if fundamentalism were true. But that is the conclusion you call absurd, without giving any reason for it. Now since you will not give a reason for *that*, I shall try another opening into the inner chamber of understanding that is walled around by this argument. The second premise may be a door. Let us examine it, if you will. How do you know that only a few are born again, whatever that means?

Bertha: The polls all say so.

Socrates: This thing of being born again—does it take place inside us or outside us?

Bertha: Inside us. In the heart, or soul.

Socrates: And do the polls measure the heart or soul?

Bertha: No.

Socrates: Then how can the polls know how many are really born again?

Bertha: They can't, I guess. But I still disagree with the fundamentalists' narrowness. That's the bottom line. Who do they think they are to say who goes to heaven?

Socrates: That would seem to be an extremely important question, at any rate, would it not?—how to get to heaven? how to have a happy eternity?

Bertha: Yes . . .

Socrates: So we ought to try to find the true answer to it, perhaps above all others.

Bertha: Now you're starting to sound like one of them.

Socrates: If that's what *they* are—people who ask that question—then it would seem that they are only reasonable, and those who do *not* ask that question are foolish and narrow.

Bertha: No, let's ask the question. I'm broad-minded. I'll entertain any question.

Socrates: Good. Now how should we find the answer to such a question? Have you ever been in heaven?

Bertha: Of course not.

Socrates: Then it does not yet lie within your experience.

Bertha: No.

Socrates: When we want to find the truth about a matter that does not lie within our experience, what do we do?

Bertha: I don't know what you mean.

Socrates: When we want to find out what it feels like to be rich, what do we do?

Bertha: We ask someone who is rich, of course.

Socrates: Not your fellow students here?

Bertha: No.

Socrates: And when we want to find out how one makes a great poem, what do we do?

Bertha: We ask a great poet.

Socrates: Not this New Yuck *Times* that I have under my arm?

Bertha: No. That's not poetry.

Socrates: And when we want to find out how to travel in Egypt, whom do we ask?

Bertha: An Egyptian.

Socrates: Not the polls?

Bertha: No, that would be silly. Why are you asking these questions?

Socrates: To find a principle. Do you see it?

Bertha: I suppose you mean that when we want to know the truth about something that is not in our experience, we ask the expert, the one who does know by experience.

Socrates: Exactly. Well, then, when you want to know how to get to heaven, is there anyone you can ask?

Bertha: I don't know.

Socrates: What a pity. What subject did you say you studied here?

Bertha: Christianity.

Socrates: And what is that?

Bertha: Christianity is our religion.

Socrates: Why is it called "Christianity"?

Bertha: It was founded by Jesus, who is also called "Christ."

Socrates: This Jesus—would you say he was a fundamentalist?

Bertha: Certainly not!

Socrates: Is he your expert on heaven and how to get there?

Bertha: If anyone is, he is, yes.

Socrates: More than the polls, or the *Times*, or your fellow students?

Bertha: Of course.

Socrates: So if there should be a difference of opinion about this matter, Jesus would be the more reliable authority?

Bertha: Well, yes . . .

Socrates: Now what is Jesus' answer to our question how to get to heaven?

Bertha: Oh, but that is a matter of great dispute. There are many different theological schools of thought, many different denominations and churches, and no one simple answer that all agree with. It is a question of interpretation. And I believe we should be as open-minded and as broad-minded as possible. Freedom of interpretation, that's what I insist on. What Jesus meant is far from simple. We each need to interpret it in our own way.

Socrates: Oh. Then this Jesus was not a common man, a man of the people, who spoke to and for ordinary people?

Bertha: Oh, but he was. He did.

Socrates: Then he was not a good teacher?

Bertha: He was that too. Why do you ask that?

Socrates: A good teacher is one who communicates effectively, wouldn't you say? One who makes himself understood?

Bertha: Yes.

Socrates: Well, apparently this Jesus fellow was not a very effective teacher, if his present-day disciples disagree so much about the most important element of his teaching, how to get to heaven.

Bertha: As I said, it's a matter of interpretation.

Socrates: But surely there is a prior question: what did he say? Before we interpret a saying, we must know the saying. Tell me, did he say that there were many different ways to heaven, or only one? Did he say his way was one among many, or the only one?

Bertha: Oh. Well, he said, "I am the way, the truth, and the life; no one can come to the Father but by me." But what he meant by that, I think, was . . .

Socrates: May we first see what he said before we investigate what he may have meant?

Bertha: What good would that do if we didn't understand it? Why parrot his words if we don't know how to interpret them correctly? That's what the fundamentalists do.

Socrates: Tell me, do you think we should be scientific in our attitude toward your Scriptures?

Bertha: Oh, yes. It's the fundamentalists who are unscientific, and suspicious of science, especially when applied to Scripture. Why, you should hear the nasty things they say about higher criticism . . .

Socrates: One thing at a time, please. We are not even up to lower criticism yet, only data gathering. May we look further at the data? Did this Jesus fellow say that the way to heaven was broad and easy and that many people would find it?

Bertha: Actually, he said the opposite. But that doesn't mean . . .

Socrates: Excuse me for interrupting again, but may we collect our data first before we interpret it? Perhaps you were about to speak something true, even importantly true, but truth too has a structure and an order, does it not? Should we not know the thing interpreted before we know the interpretation?

Bertha: All right.

Socrates: Now did Jesus speak of this thing the fundamentalists speak of, this being born again?

Bertha: Yes.

Socrates: What exactly did he say about it in connection with entering heaven?

Bertha: Well, he said, "Unless you are born again, you cannot see the kingdom of God."

Socrates: I see—I think. Does "seeing" here mean "entering"?

Bertha: I think so.

Socrates: And is "the kingdom of God" the same as heaven?

Bertha: I think so.

Socrates: Then Jesus and the fundamentalists seem to say the same thing on this most important question. You apparently do not agree with either of the two. What do you say instead?

Bertha: I say everyone who is sincere is accepted by God. My God is not a judge, a discriminator.

Socrates: And Jesus? Is the God he believes in a judge? Does he discriminate between the saved and the damned, according to the teachings of Jesus?

Bertha: Well, Jesus did tell a number of parables about the Last Judgment, yes, but . . . but Jesus just couldn't have been a fundamentalist. That's for sure.

Socrates: That seems to be your unquestioned and unquestionable premise. All right, then, let us summarize the whole matter in short. We seem to have three propositions here, and one of them, at least, must be false. First, that Jesus is not a fundamentalist. Second, that Jesus taught that you have to be born again to get to heaven. Third, that fundamentalism is the teaching that you have to be born again to get to heaven. Do you see that one of these propositions must be false?

Bertha: Yes.

Socrates: Now, which one? There are three ways out of this trilemma: yours, the one that seems to be the fundamentalists,' and mine.

Bertha: What are they?

Socrates: Here is your way, if I am not mistaken. You assume, first, that Jesus cannot possibly be a fundamentalist . . .

Bertha: Yes . . .

Socrates: And you say, secondly, that fundamentalism is the teaching that you must be born again to get to heaven.

Bertha: Yes.

Socrates: So your conclusion must be to deny that Jesus taught this teaching.

Bertha: Actually, you're right. I do question the authenticity of the Fourth Gospel.

Socrates: I will not ask what that means right now. A second way out of the trilemma is the fundamentalists' way, if I am not mistaken. That is to assume, first, that Jesus did teach the doctrine that you have to be born again to get to heaven, and second, that this doctrine is fundamentalism, and thus to conclude that Jesus is a fundamentalist.

Bertha: Right. What's your third way?

Socrates: I have no reason to disagree with either of my two sources, yourself or your Scriptures, since I do not claim to know more than you do or more than they do. So I accept my first premise from you, that Jesus is not a fundamentalist, and my second premise from your Scriptures, that Jesus taught the "born again" doctrine, so I conclude that the "born again" doctrine is *not* the same as fundamentalism. So we have not succeeded in defining the term we set out to define, it seems.

Bertha: Oh.

Socrates: So would you please begin again and try to define this term for me?

Bertha: No.

Socrates: No?

Bertha: No, I'm not in the market for a headache, and I feel one coming on. I'm going home to take some aspirin. You set my head spinning like a top.

Socrates: Alas, the same old story. Again I am disappointed in love.

Bertha [perking up]: Love?

Socrates: The love of wisdom. Philosophy. You ought to try it some time. It may work better than aspirin. But be prepared for disappointments, as I think you are not. The beloved is very elusive. But then, so is the God, as I have always believed. I hope I am here to learn more about the pursuit of this hidden God.

Bertha: Somehow I feel insulted.

Socrates: I was trying to help both of us.

Bertha: Well, you didn't help me. My thoughts were progressing quite nicely until you came along and confused me. You do more regress than progress for me.

Socrates: Oh, but regress can be progress.

Bertha: How can that be?

Socrates: When we are going down a wrong road. And are there not many wrong roads of the mind, just as there are many wrong roads for the body in the world?

Bertha: But where do you turn when you get stuck in the mud?

Socrates: If I may make a suggestion, might it not be a good idea if you reconsulted your expert?

Bertha: Jesus, you mean?

Socrates: Yes. I am interested in learning more about him, if he is indeed the expert. Might it not be possible that he is right about the way to heaven rather than the polls or the *Times* or your school friends? Just a possibility, you understand, but it seems reasonable to at least consider it, doesn't it? At least if you are as broad-minded as you claim to be?

Bertha: Some other time, Socrates.

Socrates: I will have to accept your rain check, then, Bertha. I only hope we will finish our very serious game some time before I am removed from here, for my sake, and some time before you are removed from here, for your sake.

Bertha: Removed from here?

Socrates: Where our roads lead after death, I do not know. I thought I knew where mine would lead, and it turned out I was quite wrong. I hope the same does not happen to you, or something even worse. Before we venture on an unknown road, it would seem only prudent to consult a map, and if this Jesus you speak of claims to offer a map, I want very much to see it. Would you tell me more about it soon?

Bertha: Maybe tomorrow, Socrates.

4 Candy Confessions

Socrates meets Bertha Broadmind outside a classroom at Have It Divinity School.

Bertha Broadmind: Well, Socrates, here we are, ready for your first class at Have It Divinity School. Are you excited?

Socrates: At the prospect of learning? Yes, indeed, as I have always been. As a starving man is excited by the prospect of food.

Bertha: If you're the real Socrates, you're far from starving. You're supposed to be one of the wisest men in the world.

Socrates: Only because I know that I'm starving. If you know me, you must know the riddle of the oracle that made me me. Do you remember?

Bertha: Of course. The oracle declared you the wisest man in the world because you alone knew that you knew nothing.

Socrates: No, that's not quite right . . .

Bertha: That's what Plato said in the *Apology*.

Socrates: No, it isn't. I read that account. It's a little dressed up, of course, but it's more accurate than yours.

Bertha: How?

Socrates: On four counts. First, I did not receive the message from the oracle. My friend Chairephon did. He asked the oracle about me, and I got the message through him. I think that was the god's way of testing my trust in my friend as well as my trust in him—at least that's my guess. Second, the oracle didn't say I was wiser than anyone else, only that no one else was wiser than I. I interpreted that to mean that anyone in the world could also rise to a wisdom equal to mine simply by learning the one lesson I had learned: that I am not wise. Third, the oracle did not supply the *because*, the reason, but left it for me to find out, as a riddle. How could the man with no wisdom be the wisest? I spent the rest of my life looking for a wise man, and developed the so-called Socratic method as a result. The oracle's riddle was itself good Socratic method: a question without an answer. *I* had to find the answer. So it was really the oracle, or the god of the oracle, that was the origin of what you call philosophy, and for the crime of being a philosopher I was executed as an atheist. Fourth, my answer was not that I knew that I had no knowledge, but no wisdom. We all have some knowledge, but wisdom is a divine attribute. God alone is wise and has given to men the pursuit of wisdom, philosophy.

Bertha: Wow! That was quite a mouthful, Socrates. I was wrong in four ways! Oh, speaking of mouthfuls, I want to get a candy bar before class. Here, let me show you something I'll bet you never saw before. See, I put the money in this machine, and out comes sweetness!

Socrates: The Form of Sweetness can be purchased for a fee?

Bertha: You know what I mean. Here, taste this.

Socrates [tasting]: It is delicious indeed. Perhaps I shall come to believe in Progress after all. We had nothing like this in my day.

Bertha: The only problem is that they're awfully fattening. And both of us ought to reduce.

Socrates: Why?

Bertha: Why, because we're both too fat, of course.

Socrates: Too fat for what?

Bertha: Too fat to be good-looking, I guess.

Socrates: In my day, fat people were often considered good-looking, and were envied because only the rich could afford fattening foods. How fashions change!

Bertha: But that's progress too, Socrates, not just a change of fashion. We know through modern medicine that obesity often causes early death, especially via heart disease. To be too fat isn't good for you.

Socrates: I did not know that. You have made progress indeed. The rules of health, unlike fashions, do not change, and you have progressed in knowing them, it seems. So we should not be eating this candy if it's fattening. We should practice the virtue of moderation, or temperance, or self-control . . . You know, there's no satisfactory translation of *sophrosyne* in your language.

Bertha: I know what you mean, but let's just forget the virtues today and do it, even though we know we shouldn't. Come on, it's almost time for class to begin.

Socrates: But class is already beginning for me, right here. Your last remark is sweeter to me even than that wonderful candy bar, because it promises food for the soul if we only taste it. You have said something I have long believed to be impossible, and I would dearly love to explore this impossible thing to see if it may prove possible after all.

Bertha: But we'll miss class.

Socrates: If we go into that little room with the others and listen to a lecture, we will miss class indeed—the class we are already having. Don't you have a saying something like this—a bird in the hand is worth two in the tree?

Bertha: Yes, and somehow I think you're a more interesting teacher than Professor Nuance, anyway. All right, what do you want to explore?

Socrates: I have always believed and taught that all evil comes from ignorance, that it is impossible to truly know what is good and what is evil and nevertheless to choose the evil rather than the good. But now you said that you knew that this candy was not good for you, and yet you chose it anyway. It seems, therefore, that you have just done the impossible.

Bertha: Don't you believe in evil, Socrates?

Socrates: Of course I do. The word would not exist if it didn't mean something.

Bertha: Then how do you account for evil? Why do we choose evil?

Socrates: When we think it is really good.

Bertha: Like the candy bar?

Socrates: Yes. You chose it because it was sweet, and sweetness is good, or seems good, doesn't it?

Bertha: Yes.

Socrates: But seeming and being are not the same, are they?

Bertha: No.

Socrates: And what is that power called by which we distinguish between these two, between seeming and being?

Bertha: Knowledge, discrimination.

Socrates: So it was your lack of knowledge, which looked only at the seeming and not at the being, that accounts for your choice of this evil, this thing that was not good for you.

Bertha: No, that's not right. I knew perfectly well that the candy bar was not good for me. I chose it anyway.

Socrates: So it seems. Let us explore this mystery. Why do you think you did this thing which you said you knew was not good for you?

Bertha: I'm only human, Socrates.

Socrates: I could have guessed that. You hardly look like a god.

Bertha: So I'm imperfect.

Socrates: Is that your explanation for choosing evil? Imperfection equals evil?

Bertha: I think so, yes.

Socrates: Let's test your thought. Take this little tree here in this pot. Would you call it imperfect?

Bertha: Yes. It's small and scrawny.

Socrates: Would you call it *evil?*

Bertha: No, it just has a lot of growing to do.

Socrates: Then imperfection is not the same as evil.

Bertha: No.

Socrates: Then what is the factor we're missing, if not ignorance and not imperfection? What accounts for evil? What must be present for evil to be present? What is the cause of evil?

Bertha: That's a very hard question, Socrates. I don't know.

Socrates: I think you have answered this hard question just now.

Bertha: What do you mean?

Socrates: When you said "I don't know." That is the cause of evil. Ignorance.

Bertha: But I *did* know the candy was bad for me.

Socrates: Then why did you eat it?

Bertha: I told you. It was sweet.

Socrates: But sweetness is good, not bad.

Bertha: Yes.

Socrates: So you ate it as an apparent good.

Bertha: But I also knew it was a real evil for me. I had knowledge. I know modern medicine.

Socrates: This is a mystery indeed.

Bertha: I even knew that God didn't want me to do it, but I still did it. It was probably a sin.

Socrates: Now we are explaining one mystery by another. That word *sin*, now—I think I do not quite understand it.

Bertha: Oh, I don't either. In fact, it's probably a myth.

Socrates: Sin is a myth?

Bertha: I think so.

Socrates: But what does it mean? Even myths have meaning.

Bertha: It means deliberately disobeying God.

Socrates: And do you believe in God?

Bertha: Some sort of a God, yes.

Socrates: And do you think this God wants you to take care of your body?

Bertha: Yes.

Socrates: And eating fattening foods is disobeying the will of this God for you, then, is it not?

Bertha: Yes.

Socrates: Then it is a sin. So sin is not a myth. It exists. We just saw one.

Bertha: It was such a little one, though.

Socrates: This little tree is very little, but it is still a tree, is it not?

Bertha: Yes.

Socrates: So a little sin is still a sin, and not something else.

Bertha: Yes.

Socrates: But you said sin was a myth.

Bertha: I guess what I meant was that God was forgiving. I believe God accepts me as I am. That's why I accept myself as I am.

Socrates: You mean he doesn't want you to grow wiser or better?

Bertha: No, I don't mean that.

Socrates: Then what do you mean?

Bertha: I mean God loves us all.

Socrates: But how does this entail the conclusion that sin is a myth?

Bertha: Love forgives.

Socrates: Oh, but if I say "I forgive you," that assumes there is something to be forgiven, does it not?

Bertha: Yes.

Socrates: Then forgiveness assumes that sin is a reality, not a myth.

Bertha: I thought it was you who didn't believe in sin.

Socrates: I said I didn't think I understood its meaning. How could I disbelieve in something I didn't understand? Now perhaps if I understood something more about the God you believe in, I could understand something about the sin you don't believe in. Do you think that is so? Shall we follow that line of investigation?

Bertha: Yes.

Socrates: Well, then, this God of yours is forgiving, you say?

Bertha: Yes.

Socrates: He forgives sins?

Bertha: Yes.

Socrates: And sins are offenses against his will? Disobedience?

Bertha: Yes. You understand sin after all.

Socrates: No, I understand the concept, but I think I do not understand the reality.

Bertha: Neither do I. Especially, I don't understand how so many Christians believe in divine punishment, and hell, and judgment. You're lucky to be here at Have It instead of some place like Bobby Jo Bible School, you know, where they still teach that stuff.

Socrates: Why?

Bertha: Why, because it's a horrible, awful idea, that's why.

Socrates: But is it true?

Bertha: What?

Socrates: I said, is it true? Why the surprise? It's a simple question.

Bertha: People here don't ask simple questions like that very often, Socrates.

Socrates: Then perhaps I would be better off at Billy Jo Bible School after all. Or perhaps I was sent as a kind of missionary to this place, to teach you to ask simple questions like that.

Bertha: All right, Socrates, I'll answer your simple question. No, it's not true.

Socrates: Thank you. And how do you know that?

Bertha: Because I believe God is loving and forgiving.

Socrates: And therefore he is not also just and punishing?

Bertha: Yes. I mean, no. Well, I don't know about the *therefore*. I know what you're going to say: that it doesn't logically follow from God's mercy, that he's not also just.

Socrates: And then you were going to say in reply . . . ?

Bertha: If we keep on this way, I can hold the whole conversation with myself, and I won't need you anymore.

Socrates: That is precisely my function: to make myself dispensable.

Bertha: I don't know what I was going to reply. I just know God is loving, that's all.

Socrates: Let us try another road, then. How do you know God is loving?

Bertha: That's the whole point of Christianity, of Christ.

Socrates: And how do you know about this Christ?

Bertha: The Bible.

Socrates: You believe the Bible, then.

Bertha: Well, actually I think it's mostly myth.

Socrates: Like sin.

Bertha: Yes. But the Bible has some great moral lessons, just as your mythology did.

Socrates: And this Jesus—the Bible tells you what he said?

Bertha: Yes.

Socrates: And he said that God is loving and forgiving?

Bertha: Yes.

Socrates: Why don't you think *that's* only mythology?

Bertha: Hmmm! I don't know, I never thought about that, I guess. I just believe it, that's all. I agree with it there.

Socrates: You mean you agree with the Bible when the Bible agrees with you, but not when it doesn't.

Bertha: I don't disagree with the Bible. I just interpret some parts as myth.

Socrates: The parts you don't agree with.

Bertha: You make it sound dishonest. I just interpret it in light of my own honest convictions.

Socrates: But shouldn't you interpret any book, and any one else's words, in light of *their* convictions instead of yours? When you're interpreting, you want to know what *they* believe, don't you? Then you decide whether you believe it or not. But if you don't know what it is, what the other person believes, how can you know whether you agree or disagree with it?

Bertha: You mean we shouldn't interpret a book in light of our beliefs?

Socrates: Of course not! That confuses two things, interpretation and belief.

Bertha: Oh . . .

Socrates: Furthermore, if you do that, why do you need the Bible at all?

Bertha: What do you mean?

Socrates: If it agrees with you, it's superfluous, and if it doesn't, it's wrong. Why read a book that must be either superfluous or wrong? In fact, why read or listen to anyone? They must all be superfluous or wrong.

Bertha: That's ridiculous.

Socrates: My point exactly.

Bertha: I mean, it's ridiculous to think I was doing that.

Socrates: But if you interpret another person's words in the light of your own beliefs, that's exactly what you're doing.

Bertha: I'm confused. The simple point is that God is forgiving.

Socrates: But why do you believe that?

Bertha: If I say the Bible again, we're back in our circle.

Socrates: Well, is there any other reason? Do you think you can prove that by reason, without the Bible or Jesus?

Bertha: Hmmm. There are a lot of arguments for the existence of God . . .

Socrates: Do any of them prove that God is forgiving?

Bertha: Let's see. There are the cosmological arguments, the arguments from nature. But nature is unforgiving, so those arguments can't prove God forgives, only that he exists, and designs, and causes nature. And history—history is as unforgiving as nature, I guess. Crime and punishment. Oh, how about the moral argument, the argument from conscience? That proves more. That proves that God is good.

Socrates: But conscience is as unrelenting as nature, is it not? Does conscience prove that God forgives?

Bertha: I guess not.

Socrates: Do you have any argument that proves God forgives?

Bertha: No.

Socrates: So the only way you know God forgives is through Jesus and the Bible.

Bertha: Yes.

Socrates: And do these two sources say anything about God's punishment, and about justice and judgment, and about hell?

Bertha: Yes.

Socrates: All three things are taught in the Bible?

Bertha: Yes.

Socrates: Does Jesus teach all three things too?

Bertha: Well, yes, in parables, but I interpret this as . . .

Socrates: As myth?

Bertha: Yes.

Socrates: Then why don't you interpret Jesus' teaching that God is loving and forgiving as myth too?

Bertha: I just can't believe God is unforgiving.

Socrates: I know *what* you believe, I don't know *why* you believe it. So far all I can figure out is that the very same authority which is your only basis for believing in God's forgiveness also teaches his judgment. Isn't that true?

Bertha: Yes, but . . .

Socrates: But you accept divine mercy and deny divine judgment because you interpret the second as myth.

Bertha: Yes.

Socrates: But the only reason you do that, in turn, is because a literal divine judgment contradicts your beliefs.

Bertha: Yes.

Socrates: And I still don't know *why* you believe what you believe.

Bertha: I just do, that's all. Maybe it's irrational. Maybe we choose to believe things and choose to do things for other reasons than rational reasons. Didn't you ever think of that?

Socrates: Like eating that candy bar, for instance?

Bertha: Yes. I think you're wrong when you teach that evil comes only from ignorance. That's rationalism. That assumes that reason always rules. It doesn't. It gets pushed around by the desires and the will sometimes.

Socrates: I think you are convincing me of just that. In fact, I think I have seen two instances of it just this morning— instances of something I disbelieved in until now.

Bertha: Two instances?

Socrates: Yes. Your candy bar and your beliefs. You choose both not because they are good for you, or because they are true, but because they are sweet. Your belief that God forgives but does not judge is rather like a candy bar, is it not? It is a sweet thought, the thought that we have only half of justice to deal with when we deal with God, that God rewards goodness but does not punish evil—is not that thought sweet and desirable? And are you not attracted to it just as you are attracted to the candy bar?

Bertha: Socrates, you're a real bother, you know. First you took my class lecture away from me—a nice, comfortable listening session with Professor Nuance. Then you made me feel bad about eating that candy bar. And now you take my certainty away too, and maybe some of my beliefs as well. You give nothing, Socrates, nothing but trouble; you only take things away.

Socrates: Yes, that is true. But that too can be a service, when you need to diet rather than to eat, can it not? Perhaps your mind is overstuffed with comfortable beliefs just as your body is stuffed with sweet foods. In that case, I would be doing for you a most important service by taking your fat from you.

Bertha: I thought you said people envied the fat in your day.

Socrates: People in my day were no wiser than people in your day, Bertha. Perhaps less so. Perhaps that is why I am here. But I have not yet learned much wisdom. I think it is time I started studying your wise man, Jesus.

Bertha: If we hurry, we can get to the next class on time. You might hear about him there.

Socrates: He is the one who assures us that God is forgiving?

Bertha: Yes.

Socrates: And he is the same one who also speaks of divine justice and judgment?

Bertha: Yes, judgment upon sin.

Socrates: I must hear about this thing sin. I think I may have overlooked something very important when I identified evil with ignorance. Perhaps the truth is not that ignorance is the cause of evil, but that evil is the cause of ignorance, of willfully ignoring the truth—truths like the medical evidence about candy bars and the biblical evidence about divine punishment.

Bertha: Are you saying you don't think God is forgiving?

Socrates: Certainly not. How would I know that? I do not claim to know about this God of yours. I am here to learn, not to teach.

Bertha: Well, let me teach you one thing, Socrates, one thing I know for sure. God is love, not judgment. God is a still, small voice, not an earthquake.

Socrates: I will not ask you now just how you know that. But I will ask you this: why could God not be both?

Bertha: How could that be?

Socrates: Does not love make its own judgments? Has love no eyes? And is love not like an earthquake as well as like a still, small voice? In fact, is not love the greatest earthquake?

Bertha: I don't know what God you believe in, but I prefer a God of peace.

Socrates: Oh, but surely the first question is not what you prefer but what is the truth?

Bertha: The question is what God I choose to believe in.

Socrates: But do you choose your beliefs as you choose your candy bars?

Bertha [confused]: No, of course not . . . I don't know anymore . . .

Socrates: Ah, the magic words!

Bertha: But I do know that we've missed our class.

Socrates: But we did not miss the whole purpose of a class: learning. I, at least, have learned something about the relationship between evil and ignorance that I did not know before. And I think perhaps you also have learned something you did not know before—about the relation between belief and the God you believe in? Or at least about not knowing what you thought you knew?

Bertha: I must admit I learned *that*, your good old Lesson One again. Thanks for the free class.

Socrates: Oh, it was not free. It is never free. Whenever we learn something new, we pay for it with something old.

Bertha: What do you mean by that?

Socrates: We must give up ignorance and prejudice and falsehood if we are to gain truth. To add a new idea to the mind, we must eject an old one. So all learning is subtracting as well as adding, dying as well as birthing. You see, the mind is rather like a hotel, and I am only its janitor, not a guest. My service is only to help clean out the rooms for the guests to fit into—oh, speaking of janitors, there's my friend Flanagan again! And there he goes again, as quickly as before. Do you know that man, Bertha?

Bertha: What man?

Socrates: Didn't you see that tall, gray-haired janitor? He passed right in front of you.

Bertha: No, Socrates, I think you're seeing things.

Socrates: Of course I'm seeing things. I'm not blind.

Bertha: Oops! Look at the time. If I don't go now, I'll be late for my next class too. Socrates, I'll see you tomorrow in Professor Shift's Comparative Religions class. Where are you headed now?

Socrates: To a class called Science and Religion.

Bertha: Oh, good. My friend Thomas Keptic is in that class. Be sure you get to meet him and tell him hello from me. You'll like him, Socrates. He asks almost as many questions as you do. Bye! See you tomorrow!

5 Are Miracles Unscientific?

Socrates and Thomas Keptic are walking out of Professor Flatland's first class in the course Science and Religion.

Thomas: Well, Socrates, what did you think of that lecture? Wasn't it brilliant?

Socrates: Yes, indeed it was.

Thomas: Then why do you look so disappointed?

Socrates: Brilliant lectures often disappoint me—not because they are brilliant but because they are lectures.

Thomas: Oh, I think I see. You'd prefer Socratic method, right?

Socrates: Yes. I miss the opportunity to ask the professor some of the many questions that are bothering me.

Thomas: Why *didn't* you ask any questions?

Socrates: I thought it improper to interrupt such a brilliant performance.

Thomas: Are you being sarcastic?

Socrates: Not at all. His lecture helped me to catch up on one important aspect of the 2386 years of the history of human thought that I've missed. I found it nothing short of amazing to hear him whiz through the centuries like that. Oh, I enjoyed his lecture, all right, but I was disappointed that the most important question about the relationship between science and religion was not even touched.

Thomas: How can you say that? You don't know anything about what's been happening in those 2386 years. Professor Flatland covered all the important developments.

Socrates: Perhaps so, but the question I missed was not a development. I mean *truth.* Surely it is more important to know whether what a man says is true or false than to know when he said it or to whom he said it.

Thomas: I'm sure the professor would be willing to argue any question with you, Socrates. Perhaps later in the course.

Socrates: I hope so.

Thomas: You don't sound very hopeful.

Socrates: To be frank, I think it unlikely that my hope will be fulfilled.

Thomas: Why?

Socrates: Because such a fulfillment depends on two unlikely events—the professor changing his classroom method from lecture to discussion, and my being allowed to remain here until he does.

Thomas: Allowed? I don't understand. Who . . . ?

Socrates: Why, there's the professor now! Perhaps he would allow me to approach him with my questions now. That's not improper here, is it?

Thomas: Certainly not.

Socrates: I should hope not. How could it ever be improper to ask a man to help you to find the truth? Oh, Professor Flatland!

Flatland: Yes?

Socrates: I admired the lecture you just gave on the history of opinions concerning the relationship between religion and science. But I have a question on my mind that keeps bothering me, and I was hoping you could help me to answer it.

Flatland: I'd be glad to try. Hello there, Thomas.

Thomas: Hello, Professor. I'd like you to meet my friend Socrates.

Flatland: What a wonderful costume! Hello, "Socrates."

Socrates: Hello.

Thomas: Socrates, Professor Flatland has answered more of my questions than anyone else I've ever met. I'm confident he'll be able to answer yours.

Flatland: That's a very nice compliment, Thomas, but really, now, I think of my function more as raising questions than answering them.

Thomas: That's true, Professor. Before I took your course, I was naive. I believed in all sorts of things, including miracles.

Socrates: That is precisely my question, Professor—miracles. I think it is a question more important, even, than any of the many questions you covered in your lecture, complete as it was. Do miracles ever really happen? And how do you know whether they do or not? How can we find the truth about this question?

Flatland: A very good question, Socrates. But I thought my lecture today covered it pretty completely.

Socrates: I must have failed to understand it, then, for I thought it did not cover it at all. I thought your lecture covered only the history of opinions about the relation between science and religion.

Flatland: Yes, and about the miraculous and the supernatural. I tried to show how belief in miracles always arises in prescientific ages and disappears in scientific ages like our own. The point, I thought, was quite simple and obvious.

Socrates: Alas, I fear you must have a real dunderhead on your hands, Professor. For I do not see how it logically follows from the fact that many people today no longer believe in miracles, that miracles never happen.

Flatland: That's not what I mean.

Socrates: Oh, good. I was hoping I misunderstood you.

Flatland: Why?

Socrates: Because *that* argument must assume that whatever most people cease to believe in never existed—a very strange assumption indeed, for it would mean that we can change the world just by changing our beliefs, and even that we can change the past.

Flatland: Change the past?

Socrates: Yes, if you argue that miracles never happened in the past because scientific people in the present have ceased to believe in them.

Thomas: Socrates, that's not fair. You're making the professor's argument look silly.

Socrates: I meant to do the opposite—to clearly separate him from the silly, not to implicate him in it.

Flatland: Thank you, Socrates. No, that's not my argument. Rather, it's the argument from science. It's not just the change in opinions that has disproved miracles; it's the progress in science. Science deals with facts, not just opinions.

Socrates: I see. So science has disproved miracles?

Flatland: Yes.

Socrates: Which science?

Flatland: Eh?

Socrates: Which science has disproved miracles? And how? By what experiment, or discovery, or proof? And which scientist made this discovery, and when?

Flatland: Oh, well now, that's quite a whole host of questions.

Socrates: Yes. Well?

Flatland: But of course we can't point to a *single* scientific discovery that disproves miracles . . .

Socrates: You can't point to a single scientific discovery that disproves miracles? And yet you say science has disproved miracles?

Flatland: It is more than any one discovery. It is the whole scientific attitude, the whole scientific climate of opinion . . .

Socrates: I thought we were beyond a mere change in opinions. Aren't we now regressing back to the silly argument that you repudiated? I thought science dealt with specific facts and proofs and experiments and discoveries.

Flatland: It does.

Socrates: Then please tell me which ones have disproved miracles. To begin with, which science?

Flatland: Science itself.

Socrates: With a capital *S?*

Flatland: Yes, if you will.

Socrates: I do not will that. It sounds more like religion than science to me.

Flatland: Socrates, let me try to explain. People used to believe in miracles only because they didn't know the true scientific explanations for natural events. Now that we know them, there's no need to believe in miracles anymore. For instance, people in your culture believed in an angry god they called Zeus who hurled down thunderbolts from the sky, didn't they?

Socrates: Some did, yes.

Flatland: And that was only because they didn't know about electrical energy. Now that we know what really makes lightning, no one believes in Zeus anymore. People used to think diseases were caused by demons, until they discovered germs. People used to think the sun was a god, until astronomy discovered that it was a gas.

Socrates: So no one believes in the gods anymore?

Flatland: Not those gods, the gods of natural phenomena.

Socrates: I don't see why not. I don't see how your science has refuted them. I don't see why some people couldn't believe in both your science and our gods. For instance, take Zeus. Now if I were Zeus, I might well use electrical energy to cast down my thunderbolts. And if I were a demon, I might well use germs to cause diseases. And as for the sun . . .

Flatland: Are you serious?

Socrates: Certainly. Why not?

Flatland: This is ridiculous, especially for you, you who are supposed to be a rational philosopher.

Socrates: Why?

Flatland: We just don't need the gods anymore to explain nature.

Socrates: And therefore the gods do not exist? I don't see how that logically follows.

Flatland: Look here. Take Apollo. Apollo was an early symbol for the sun. We no longer need that symbol; we just refer to the sun itself.

Socrates: Are you sure it wasn't the other way round? Are you sure early man didn't see the sun as a symbol for Apollo?

Flatland: But we know what the sun is. It's not a god; it's a gas, a ball of fire.

Socrates: Gas may be what the sun is *made of*. But what it *is*, now, that's another question, isn't it? If the sun *were* a god, couldn't his body be made of gas or fire? Perhaps what we see is not Apollo himself but his body, or his chariot.

Flatland: I see. You're using Aristotle's distinction between formal and material causes.

Socrates: Call it what you will, the distinction is necessary, is it not? A poem, for instance, may be made *of* words, but it's made *into* a poem, it *is* a poem, and not just words, is it not? And you, Professor—are you *made of* flesh and bones, or *are* you flesh and bones?

Flatland: Do you really believe the sun *is* a god named Apollo? How dogmatic! How naive! How . . . metaphysical!

Socrates: I do not know whether the sun is a god or not. But apparently you do know. So it is you who are dogmatic. And it is you who are the metaphysician, for you claim to know what the sun's very essence is—gas—while I do not.

Flatland: I'm not claiming knowledge of metaphysics, just knowledge of science. Science has made the gods gratuitous.

Socrates: And therefore they do not exist? How could you know that, unless you also know that whatever is gratuitous does not exist? But surely that is not only a thing you cannot know, it is also a thing that is not true. Many gratituous things exist, such as grace, or beauty, or generosity, or excess facial hair, or perhaps this very argument.

Flatland: All right, Socrates, perhaps science hasn't disproved the gods, but it has certainly given quite adequate explanations of nature without them. The things you ancients thought were supernatural, like the thunderbolt, we've explained as natural.

Socrates: But we did not think thunderbolts were supernatural, anymore than rainstorms.

Flatland: But you believed in miracles, didn't you?

Socrates: Many people did, yes.

Flatland: Such as . . . ?

Thomas: Oh, let's just leap to the miracles we really care about. When people argue about whether miracles really happened, they don't think of Apollo, but of Jesus. Let's talk about things like the virgin birth and the resurrection and feeding the 5000 from five loaves.

Socrates: Fine. They certainly sound like miracles to me. Now, Professor, how has your science explained these things as merely natural phenomena?

Flatland: It hasn't quite done that yet. It hasn't explained away *all* the things people thought of as miraculous yet, but it's getting there. Science is still in its infancy. In another thousand years, who knows what it will be able to explain?

Socrates: I certainly don't. Do you?

Flatland [surprised by the question]: Uh . . . no, but surely the science of the future will be to the science of the present as the science of the present is to the science of the past.

Socrates: How do you know that?

Flatland: Why, the whole movement of science is in that direction—the elimination of miracles.

Socrates: And you know that this movement will continue, and in the same direction, and to a final end of the elimination of all miracles.

Flatland: Well, of course, we can't know for certain what tomorrow will bring . . .

Socrates: And can we base a scientific argument on what we do not know?

Flatland: No.

Socrates: Then your faith in science's future elimination of miracles is not itself scientific, but more like something religious.

Flatland [brightening at a new tack]: You know, in a sense, you're right, Socrates. I do believe, in a religious way, in a lot of things: in science, for one thing, but also in miracles. Does that surprise you? I believe in real miracles. Science itself is a miracle. The true meaning of *miracle* is "wonder"— anything that excites awe and admiration. The world is full of miracles. We just don't notice them; we take them for granted. You don't need a virgin birth to have a miracle; every so-called normal birth is a miracle.

Socrates: I see. But now you are talking about something else. You are changing the meaning of the word.

Flatland: Does that bother you?

Socrates: Yes. For I find it very useful to know what a word means and to have it keep meaning the same thing, just as I find it useful to know the places on a map and to keep them where they are. How could you use a map whose names and locations kept shifting and changing places?

Flatland: Then let's just use this definition of miracle, the one I just gave you.

Socrates: But that is not what people mean by the word.

Flatland: It's what I mean. You're talking with me, not other people.

Socrates: All right, but I think there is a good reason why other people do not follow your usage here.

Flatland: What?

Socrates: You have stretched the word so thin that you have emptied it of meaning. By your definition, anything can be a miracle. But if anything is a miracle, nothing is a miracle. There is nothing to contrast with miracle. It becomes a synonym for *everything*— not a topic about which we can say anything very interesting, I think.

Flatland: But don't you see, Socrates?—every birth is a miracle, every thing is a miracle, but our eyes are dulled with familiarity. If every birth were a virgin birth, we'd call non-virgin births miraculous. If rivers ran with blood instead of water, we'd call a water river miraculous. Don't you understand my vision, see what I see, what I'm trying to show you?

Socrates: I do indeed, and I can even agree with it. What I quarrel with is only your usage. All things are wonderful, but not all things are miracles.

Flatland: We can use words any way we want. Language is our servant, not our master.

Socrates: Oh, I do not think so. But in any case, mustn't we at least use our words in the same sense as others do if we want others to understand us?

Flatland: Of course.

Socrates: Then we should use the word *miracle* as others do too. And what they mean is not a natural wonder but a supernatural wonder.

Flatland: All right, suppose I concede that point to you, just for the sake of talking your language. In the popular sense of miracle, I think nothing is a miracle. In my sense, everything is a miracle.

Socrates: So you don't believe miracles ever happen.

Flatland: In the popular sense, no. But in my sense, they happen all the time. That's why I want to use my sense. The point I want to make is basically positive, that miracles *do* happen. Why not concentrate on that, my positive point?

Socrates: Because most people would agree with it, but they would not agree with your negative point, that miracles in the popular sense don't happen.

Flatland: So?

Socrates: Do people need to be taught what they already know or what they don't know?

Flatland: What they don't know.

Socrates: And they already know your positive point, but not your negative point.

Flatland: Right.

Socrates: Therefore they need to be taught your negative point, not your positive point.

Flatland: I'm not sure they agree with my positive point. I think few people see it, really.

Socrates: Do you think most people would disagree with it, that they would say we *shouldn't* feel wonder at ordinary births, for instance?

Flatland: No, but people don't practice what they preach. They'd *say* we should feel this way, but they don't.

Socrates: Then let us remind them, by all means. But let us also enlighten them if they do not know the other thing, that supernatural miracles don't happen.

Flatland: Fine. Let's. But I thought you were defending miracles and gods and supernatural explanations. That's why I was so surprised—you of all people, defending superstition.

Socrates: I am only defending inquiry. I do not claim to know whether miracles happen or not. I questioned only your certainty that they didn't. And I still question it.

Flatland: I already told you my reason. It was easy for people to believe in miracles before the rise of the scientific world view. Once we learned that the world can be explained naturally, on its own, once we learned that the world has its own rational laws, once we stopped looking at the world as an unreliable stage set moved about at the will of arbitrary and unpredictable gods, we stopped believing in miracles. That's just a fact of history.

Socrates: Oh, now I think I understand. You think there are no miracles because the world has its own intrinsic natural laws, which science discovers.

Flatland: Yes.

Socrates: No.

Flatland: What do you mean, no?

Socrates: I mean that the opposite is true. Natural laws allow miracles, rather than disallowing them.

Flatland: How do you get that?

Socrates: Only if you believe in a world that stands on its own, a world of inherent natural laws, can there be exceptions to those laws, or miracles. The very concept of an exception to natural law, presupposes the concept of natural law. If there are no natural laws, there are no supernatural exceptions, no miracles.

Flatland: So pantheists as well as atheists can't believe in miracles, then.

Socrates: Exactly—atheists, because there's no supernature; pantheists, because there's no nature. Atheists have no God outside nature; pantheists have no nature outside God. And the concept of miracle is the concept of an outside God invading nature.

Flatland: I see. But I'm not an atheist or a pantheist, and I still don't believe in miracles. I believe in the natural order of things. That belief may *allow* miracles, as you say, but it doesn't *compel* them.

Socrates: That's right. And I still don't know why you don't believe in miracles, especially since your belief in nature allows them, at least.

Flatland: They contradict science.

Socrates: That is what I want to know. How do they contradict science?

Flatland: Why, science tells us that things like virgin births simply do not happen?

Socrates: Does science tell us what always happens, or what usually happens?

Flatland: What do you mean?

Socrates: Do the laws of your science tell you what does in fact happen, or what can happen?

Flatland: I'm not sure I understand the question.

Socrates: Are the laws of your science like the laws of mathematics? Are they necessities? Or are they descriptions of how things happen in the physical world?

Flatland: The latter.

Socrates: And things couldn't ever be different in mathematics, could they? Might two plus two become five rather than four tomorrow?

Flatland: No.

Socrates: But what happens in the physical world could be different, couldn't it? The sun might stop shining tomorrow, or explode. Or you might die.

Flatland: Yes.

Socrates: Then there can be exceptions to these laws of science: miracles.

Flatland: No, miracles are illogical.

Socrates: I thought we had just made that distinction—between the laws of logic and mathematics and the laws of nature.

Flatland: Perhaps we didn't understand each other.

Socrates: Let's try it another way. You can't even conceive of an exception to the laws of logic or math, but you can conceive of exceptions to the laws of nature.

Flatland: How's that? Give an example.

Socrates: All right. You can't conceive of a man both walking through a wall and not walking through a wall at the same time, can you?

Flatland: No.

Socrates: But you can conceive of a man walking through a wall, can't you?

Flatland: Of course not. We can't walk through walls.

Socrates: No, but we can conceive it, can't we? We can write fiction about it. We can desire to walk through walls.

Flatland: Yes. But we can no more do it than we can make two plus two equal five.

Socrates: We can't do it because of physical laws, not because of logical or mathematical laws, isn't that right?

Flatland: Yes.

Socrates: But the reason we can't both walk and not walk through a wall is because of logical laws. It's the same reason we can't both walk and not walk through an open door.

Flatland: Oh, I see. All right. So what?

Socrates: Miracles contradict physical laws, but not logical laws. If a man feeds 5000 people from 5 loaves, he does not at the same time feed 5000 people from 55 loaves. Even miracles must obey logical laws.

Flatland: I still don't see the importance of the distinction.

Socrates: It makes miracles possible, rather than impossible. Mind you, I still do not know whether they ever happen or not. But if they contradicted logical laws, if they were as illogical as you seem to think they are, then we could be certain ahead of time that they could never happen.

Flatland: They still contradict physical laws.

Socrates: Even that is not quite correct, I think.

Flatland: Why?

Socrates: Because we admitted that these physical laws were only statements about how things do in fact happen usually, didn't we?

Flatland: Yes.

Socrates: So miracles would be the unusual.

Flatland: No, more than that. Black orchids are unusual, but talking orchids are miraculous.

Socrates: A good distinction. All right, suppose we put it like this. A miracle would be like a gift of extra money to a bankbook balance. It would not contradict the balance, only add to it. Or like extra food put into a goldfish bowl or like a king's pardon to a prisoner who had been convicted by the king's court. The laws of the court, the laws of life in the goldfish bowl, and the laws of accounting, are not contradicted by the addition, just added to. Miracles would be something like that, wouldn't they?—not subtractions from natural laws but additions.

Flatland: No, they would be subtractions.

Socrates: Why?

Flatland: Because they demean the integrity of nature. A nature that God has to keep patching up and revising is not as glorious and good as a nature that God leaves on its own.

Socrates: I see. Nature must be independent, then, to be great and good and glorious?

Flatland: To be itself, to have its own identity, yes.

Socrates: Would you say that a husband demands his wife by having sexual intercourse with her?

Flatland: Of course not.

Socrates: But are not miracles like Father God impregnating Mother Nature with his life? Why should that demean her? Would it not in fact fulfill her?

Flatland: I don't think the analogy holds. Men can appreciate and love women, but supernaturalists can't really love and appreciate nature. Only naturalists can.

Socrates: I think it is just the opposite. I think only supernaturalists can love and appreciate nature.

Flatland: What? For what reason?

Socrates: For the same reason that only those who know another language than their own, or another country than their own, can appreciate their own, by contrast. For the same reason that only those who face death can appreciate life.

Flatland: You keep using analogies. I don't think they hold.

Socrates: The glue that holds them is the principle of contrast. You appreciate a thing only by contrast. Isn't that a true principle?

Flatland: Yes, it is.

Socrates: Well, then, if *nature* means simply "all there is"—well, all there is is hardly a topic about which we can feel much love or passion, is it? It means simply "everything," and "everything" has no character, no personality.

Flatland: Everything has character. Sure it does.

Socrates: Every *thing* does, yes. Every single thing. Every stone, because there are other stones. But not nature, if there is no supernatural.

Flatland: Look here, I think we're wandering from the really important issues.

Socrates: I had hoped we were wandering into them. But what do you think the really important issues about miracles are? I had thought that the important issue was whether they were true, whether they were real.

Flatland: Perhaps so, but I mean that miracles are not the essence of religion.

Socrates: Which religion?

Flatland: Any religion.

Socrates: Yours, for instance?

Flatland: Yes.

Socrates: And yours is Christianity?

Flatland: Yes.

Socrates: And your religion does speak of miracles?

Flatland: Yes.

Socrates: But you think they can be subtracted, and all the essentials would still remain?

Flatland: Yes.

Socrates: What are these miracles?

Flatland: Why, the Incarnation and the Atonement and the Resurrection, for instance.

Socrates: What do those words mean?

Flatland: Oh, I see. Socrates wouldn't know that, would he? All right, it's a good exercise. It means the supreme God became a man and died and rose from death to save us from sin and death and hell.

Socrates: And you think this is not essential? If this happened, if it really happened, how can it be simply dropped, like extra clothing? What remains?

Flatland: Timeless truths. How to live. Love.

Socrates: Ah, but everyone already knows them. If your religion amounts only to the Great Platitudes, why bother with it? Why be a Christian rather than anything else?

Flatland: I think that's a question you'd have to take up with Professor Shift in Comparative Religions.

Socrates: I was rather hoping to take it up with you, since you claimed to be a Christian. I still do not clearly know what that means.

Flatland: Perhaps I don't either. I keep questioning . . . I thought you'd approve that.

Socrates: Oh, I do. But I wonder about these stories of miracles in your holy books. It seems obviously very important to know whether they are true or false.

Flatland: I think it is very likely that they were myths added later to the text.

Socrates: Can your science prove that? Do you know enough about history and texts to *prove* that?

Flatland: Not quite yet, but we're working on it. It seems very likely, because that's what happened in most other religions in their scriptures. Myths and miracles were added later. For instance, the story of Muhammad flying to the moon on a magic horse was clearly a later addition, because the original holy book of Islam, the Koran, says that there is only one miracle in this religion, the Koran itself. And the miracles in the later stories of Buddhist saints contradicts Buddha's own teaching that no true disciple of his would perform miracles because that would encourage belief in the independent reality of nature, which Buddha taught was an illusion.

Socrates: So the miracles in this Christian holy book are like that too? They contradict something else in the book?

Flatland: Well, no, actually, they don't.

Socrates: Hmmm. And still you say they must have been added later.

Flatland: Yes.

Socrates: Why?

Flatland: Socrates, we must all interpret a book, even a holy book, in light of our own sincerely held beliefs. If you don't believe in miracles, then the most charitable interpretation of the miracle stories in the Scriptures is to accept them as myths and symbols, not to reject them as lies.

Socrates: Perhaps that is the most charitable interpretation, but it is surely not the most clear and honest one. And if it is not honest, I do not see how it can be truly charitable either.

Flatland: Why do you say it is not clear and honest?

Socrates: I think you are confusing *belief* with *interpretation*.

Flatland: No, I'm just saying we have to interpret a book in light of our beliefs.

Socrates: And I'm saying we must *not* do that.

Flatland: Why not?

Socrates: If you wrote a book to tell other people what your beliefs were, and I read it and interpreted it in light of my beliefs, which were different from yours, would you be happy?

Flatland: If you disagreed with me? Why not? You're free to make up your own mind.

Socrates: No, I said *interpreted* the book in light of my beliefs. For instance, if you wrote a book against miracles and I believed in miracles, and I interpreted your book as a defense of miracles, would you be happy?

Flatland: Of course not. That's misinterpretation.

Socrates: Even if it were my honest belief?

Flatland: Oh, I see. We have to *interpret* a book in light of the author's beliefs, and *criticize* it in light of our own.

Socrates: Precisely. Otherwise we are imposing our views on another. And that is certainly not charitable, but arrogant.

Flatland: So you're saying we have to interpret the miracle stories in the Scriptures as literal, not symbolic?

Socrates: I do not know that. I have not read them yet.

Flatland: What are you saying, then?

Socrates: That we cannot decide how to *interpret* them by consulting our own beliefs, but only by consulting them.

Flatland: I see. Then our discussion today about them can't really decide anything, if you haven't read them yet.

Socrates: It can decide whether miracles *can* happen, but not whether they *do*. It can decide whether they contradict the laws of nature, and whether they contradict the laws of logic, and whether or not we can decide whether miracles happen without looking at the evidence and reading the texts. And the answer to those questions seems to be no. So I think we have made some progress, even though we have not found out whether miracles do actually happen or not.

Flatland: I'm still a skeptic.

Socrates: Oh, so am I, if a skeptic is someone who does not know, especially if a skeptic is one who does not even know whether or not he can know. But if a skeptic is someone who thinks he does know when he really doesn't, if a skeptic is someone who thinks he *knows* that he cannot know, then I am not a skeptic. For such a skepticism is far too dogmatic for me.

Flatland: And you think that's what I am?

Socrates: I don't know, Professor. If the shoe fits, wear it. If not, throw it away. I offer myself not as professor to the professor, but only as your intellectual garbageman.

6 How to Be Comparatively Religious

Socrates and Bertha Broadmind are walking out of the first class meeting of Professor Shift's Comparative Religions course at Have It Divinity School. Socrates looks resigned. Bertha catches up to him, concerned.

Bertha: Socrates, what's wrong? Why didn't you ask any questions in there? I'm sure you're bursting with questions as usual. Why didn't you say anything? I watched you—you looked interested at first, but then sort of glum. What happened to your famous questions?

Socrates: They are still very much with me, I assure you. I was hoping for the right moment to divest myself of some of my burdens, but the moment never came.

Bertha: I don't understand. Why do you think that?

Socrates: Because for me, the moment to ask a question is the moment when there is some hope of finding an answer, or finding someone who can find an answer. What else is a question, after all, but an expressed hope for an answer?

Bertha: But Professor Shift is one of the world's most renowned scholars in comparative religions. If anyone should be able to answer your questions, it's him. But you waited too long, and the class ended.

Socrates: I don't think so, Bertha. I think, rather, that there is more hope that *you* can answer my questions, and that my class is not ended, but just beginning now.

Bertha [shocked]: Me, Socrates?

Socrates: Yes, Bertha, you. You or any one of the other students in that class.

Bertha: But there were about forty of them! Are you saying that any one of us could educate you better than Professor Shift?

Socrates: I think that is likely, yes.

Bertha: Why, for goodness' sake?

Socrates: Because of what education is—*e-ducare*, to lead out, out of the cave of prejudice and illusion. And the first and most disastrous illusion, the one I have always thought to be the greatest enemy of education, is the illusion that we know when we do not know.

Bertha: Oh, your famous "learned ignorance," Lesson One. But do you think Shift hasn't learned that lesson?

Socrates: It seemed so to me.

Bertha: Why?

Socrates: Because to learn that lesson we must pass through a narrow gate. To do that, we must stoop. To make a bad pun, one who stoops is stooped. But Professor Shift is not stupid, but brilliant. He was so full of answers that he seemed to me not to hear the questions.

Bertha: I don't think that's fair. Why do you think he didn't really hear the questions?

Socrates: Did you hear what he did with the few questions that were asked?

Bertha: Why, yes; he answered them brilliantly, I thought.

Socrates: *Too* brilliantly, I thought.

Bertha: How can someone be too brilliant?

Socrates: I think I can explain that to you. Would you agree that to give a questioner the answer he seeks, you must hear his question first?

Bertha: Of course.

Socrates: And with the heart as well as with the ears?

Bertha: What do you mean by the heart?

Socrates: I mean that you must understand the *questionableness* of the question; you must understand the uncertainty of the questioner.

Bertha: I agree with your principle, but don't you think Professor Shift understands uncertainty? He certainly speaks out against all dogma and sectarianism and provincialism.

Socrates: Yes, he *certainly* does. He reminds me too much of my old acquaintances the Sophists. They were quite certain that there was no certainty.

Bertha: You think of Shift as a Sophist? But he preaches open-mindedness. That's his main theme every class.

Socrates: Yes, he is very closed-minded about being open-minded, isn't he? Wouldn't it be more open-minded to be open-minded about everything? About being open-minded *and* about being closed-minded? Open-minded toward those who agree with him *and* open-minded about those who disagree with him about dogma and certainty and all that?

Bertha: He is open to all the religions of the world!

Socrates: Except those believers in his own who disagree with his dogma that there is no dogma—the people he calls "fundamentalists." He never actually refuted that fellow he was constantly sneering at, you know. All he did was name calling, and that's an appeal to passion and prejudice and provincialism, not to reason.

Bertha: What fellow?—Oh Jerry Fallout, you mean?

Socrates: Yes. Shift says we should listen to other religions instead of criticizing them, but he seemed to be criticizing this Fallout fellow without listening to him.

Bertha: Well, even if he doesn't perfectly practice what he preaches, who does? But you've got to agree with what he preaches, anyway.

Socrates: How can I agree with a self-contradiction?

Bertha: What self-contradiction?

Socrates: He preaches that we shouldn't preach. Did you hear the nasty things he said about preaching your religion to people? It all seemed pretty preachy to me.

Bertha: Well, I'm sorry you didn't like Shift.

Socrates: I didn't say I didn't like him. I said I didn't have much hope he could answer my questions, as I hope you can.

Bertha: Because I know so much less than he does?

Socrates: No, because you know more: that you do not know. And because you do not see questions as opportunities to show how much you know, as he did.

Bertha: I just can't believe you find Shift closed-minded. He has the reputation of being one of the most liberal professors around.

Socrates: What do you mean by *liberal?*

Bertha: Well, in comparative religions, it means seeing all religions as equal.

Socrates: And this makes him open-minded?

Bertha: Yes.

Socrates: I fail to see the connection.

Bertha: But it's so simple, Socrates. If you believe only one religion is true, then you believe that all the others that contradict it are false. Don't you see that?

Socrates: Oh, I see that very clearly, though I wonder whether Professor Shift does. But I don't see how thinking an idea is false means not being open-minded to it. How could you possibly have good reason for concluding that any idea is false unless you first listened to it? And listening to an idea—really listening—isn't that open-mindedness?

Bertha: Yes, but once you conclude that the idea is false, you no longer have an open mind. You've made up your mind to reject it.

Socrates: And you think that is bad?

Bertha: Of course. All closed-mindedness is bad.

Socrates: Closed-mindedness at the end of an investigation as well as at the beginning?

Bertha: I think we should have an open mind at all times.

Socrates: And having an open mind means always seeking?

Bertha: Yes.

Socrates: Then all that you seek is more seeking, rather than finding. For you never want to lack an open mind, and an open mind means seeking. But if you do not seek in order to find, then you do not really seek, do you? There is nothing to seek for.

Bertha: You're confusing me.

Socrates: Let me put the point differently. What do you think is the good of an open mind? What is its purpose or end?

Bertha: I guess to avoid closed-mindedness.

Socrates: That is like saying the purpose of living is to avoid dying, or that the purpose of always being cold is to avoid ever being hot. You have not told me why you seek to be open-minded rather than closed-minded.

Bertha: But I thought you knew that very well, Socrates. I always thought of you as one of the most open-minded people who ever lived.

Socrates: Perhaps I do know that very well, as you say; but I do not know whether *you* know it very well. My question was designed to find that out. What do *you* think is the purpose of open-mindedness?

Bertha: I guess I never gave it much thought, but I'm sure I'd agree with your opinion about it, Socrates. How would you answer that question?

Socrates: Very well, I will give you my answer, since you will not give me yours. But only as an aid to finding your own. And you must say whether you agree or not. I would say that the purpose of an open mind is to learn.

Bertha: Very good, Socrates, I certainly agree with that.

Socrates: Then I ask you, to learn *what?*

Bertha: Everything.

Socrates: To learn truth, or falsehood, or both, or neither?

Bertha: Both. Everything.

Socrates: To know falsehood as falsehood, or to mistakenly believe falsehood to be truth?

Bertha: To know falsehood as falsehood.

Socrates: In other words, to know the truth about falsehood.

Bertha: Yes.

Socrates: Then the only thing you want to know is truth: the truth about truth and the truth about falsehood, but not falsehood about either. Isn't that right?

Bertha: Yes.

Socrates: Then we have the same definition of open-mindedness and its purpose. Just as an open mouth is a means to the end of closing it on good food, but not poison, and an open door is a means to enable a desired guest to enter, but not a robber, so an open mind is a means to the end of learning the truth about everything, not falsehoods.

Bertha: I can't refute you, Socrates.

Socrates: Say rather that you can't refute the truth. Socrates you can refute, and should, whenever I do not speak the truth. And when I do speak it, it is not the speaker but the speech that is irrefutable. Well, now that we agree about what open-mindedness is, let us see whether we also agree about what truth is. What is truth, Bertha?

Bertha: Oh, thanks, Socrates, for the nice easy question.

Socrates: You're welcome.

Bertha: I was kidding.

Socrates: I wasn't.

Bertha: You think that was an easy question?

Socrates: I know of few that are easier.

Bertha: Well, then, please tell me what *you* think truth is, and I'll tell you whether I agree with you or not.

Socrates: Very well. Truth is simply saying what is. If you tell me what is, you tell me the truth. What could be simpler than that?

Bertha: What is falsehood, then?

Socrates: If you tell me what is not and say that it is, you tell a falsehood.

Bertha: That's the same as a lie, right?

Socrates: A lie is a deliberate falsehood. I could also tell you a falsehood not deliberately but out of ignorance.

Bertha: O.K., I agree. Now what?

Socrates: Truth and falsehood are opposed, then, are they not?

Bertha: Of course.

Socrates: So that if it is true, for instance, that there is only one God and not many, then it is false that there are many gods and not just one, isn't that so?

Bertha: That's logical, I guess. Contradictions can't both be true.

Socrates: And religions do contradict each other, don't they?

Bertha: Now that's where I don't think I agree with you, Socrates.

Socrates: But surely in the example I just gave they do. Monotheism and polytheism contradict each other, and therefore one of those religions, at least, must be false, mustn't it?

Bertha: Maybe. But all the great religions of the world are monotheistic today. *They* don't contradict each other, at least.

Socrates: But isn't it true that some of those religions believe that this God is a person, an *I*, who has a will, while others do not believe this? That is what Professor Shift said.

Bertha: It's true that Eastern religions conceive God impersonally and Western religions conceive him personally. But as Professor Shift also said, that's just a difference in our images, our models, our word pictures. All those pictures are inadequate, don't you agree?

Socrates: I agree that all our thoughts are inadequate to God, but

I do not agree that they are all pictures. Some of them are
concepts. For instance, we can picture Zeus when we say "Zeus
is God." But we cannot picture "one" when we say "God is
one."

Bertha: Socrates, did you ever hear the fable of the four blind men
and the elephant?

Socrates: No.

Bertha: Well, it goes like this. Four blind men who had never seen
an elephant before went up to one and felt it. The first man felt
its tail, and said, "An elephant is a worm." The second man felt
its side, and said, "No, an elephant is a wall." The third man felt
its leg, and said, "No, an elephant is a tree." And the fourth man
felt its trunk, and said, "You're all wrong; an elephant is a giant
snake." And the four of them argued about it all day. That's how
it is with the religions of the world, arguing about God the elephant. We know about as much about God as blind men know
about an elephant. Don't you think that's a good analogy?

Socrates: No, I don't.

Bertha: Why not?

Socrates: I do not think it fits the case well. God may indeed be
many different things, as the elephant is, and it may be that we
can only know one of them at a time. It may also be true that
we can only know images or analogies of some of the things God
is, or even all of the things God is, just as the blind men used
four different analogies for the elephant, without realizing that
they were only analogies. But the question we were talking
about was whether God has a will or not. That is like two of the
blind men arguing about whether the elephant has a trunk or
not. Whether they call it a trunk or a snake, the elephant either
has it or not.

Bertha: And you think the differences between religions is like
that?

Socrates: Some of them surely seem to be. First, whether there is
any God at all or not. If atheists are right, all religions are wrong.

Second, if atheism is wrong, whether there is only one God or many. If polytheists are right, all monotheists are wrong. Third, if polytheists are wrong, whether God has a will or not. If not, then all your Western religions that say he does are wrong. Fourth, about this Jesus fellow. As I understand it, two of the three religions in your Western world that believe God has a will—Islam and Judaism—do not believe Jesus is the Messiah, or the Son of God, whatever that means, and the third religion does. That one is your religion, Christianity, I think. Thus there seem to be fundamental contradictions between your religion and Islam, Judaism, Eastern religions, polytheism and atheism. If your religion is right, all of these other religions are wrong. It's quite simple. I don't understand how you can fail to see it.

Bertha: It may seem simple to you, but the truth just can't be that simple.

Socrates: Why not?

Bertha: Because if it is, then you'd have to be an elitist. Religions would be unequal.

Socrates: And that is your premise, that that cannot be so?

Bertha: Yes.

Socrates: May I ask you whether you have any reasons for your premise, or whether that is simply a matter of faith to you—your real religion, behind the façade of the other one?

Bertha: Yes, I have reasons. All human things are fundamentally equal, Socrates, because they're all finite and imperfect, and blends of the good and the bad. Forms of art, for instance. How silly to argue which one is best. Or political systems—whichever one works for a given time or people is best. You can't say one is simply best.

Socrates: I see. You seem to be treating one of those political systems, namely democracy, as the truth and the best, not in its own realm, politics, but in the realm of religion. But I think I see your point about all human things being fundamentally equal and relative.

Bertha: Good. You agree, then?

Socrates: Yes, except for two little things. First, is religion a thing like art or politics—a human thing?

Bertha: Of course it's a human thing. It's at the heart of human life. What else could it be?

Socrates: Its dwelling place is human, certainly. But its origin—is that human, or is it divine? Was it invented by humans?

Bertha: Of course.

Socrates: But at least three religions claim to be invented by God, don't they? Don't Islam and Judaism and Christianity all claim to be divine revelations?

Bertha: You've read the textbook for the course already, haven't you?

Socrates: Yes. Am I right?

Bertha: You're right.

Socrates: Then you disagree with the claim of these religions?

Bertha: To be divine revelations rather than human? I guess I do.

Socrates: Then why do you call yourself a Christian?

Bertha: I'm surprised at you, Socrates, stooping to personal insult!

Socrates: It is I who am surprised at you. I meant no insult, only accurate description. Why did you take it as insult?

Bertha: Forget it. *[Sulks.]* I never thought *you* would turn out to be a fundamentalist! *[Spits the word.]*

Socrates: I have yet to find out what that word means. In this place I have only heard it said in blame. I have also yet to find out just what the word *Christian* means; you seem to use it only in praise. I do not see how this kind of usage can be helpful—I mean, using the words not to describe what the things really are, but only to express how you feel about them. I need to find words that describe before I can use words to praise or blame.

Bertha: Socrates, you're getting too logical for me, O.K.? Can we please go back to your disagreement with me? You said there were two of them, right? The first was that you saw Christianity as a divine revelation instead of as a human invention?

Socrates: I did not say that. I do not know what Christianity is. I said only that it *claims* to be a divine revelation, but you treat it as a human invention, and that is why you think other religions are equal to it, since they too are only human inventions. Is that correct?

Bertha: Yes. And what was your second disagreement with me?

Socrates: That you apparently see religions as only practical things, not theoretical things.

Bertha: What do you mean by that?

Socrates: You used art and politics as analogies, rather than philosophy or science. Art and politics are for goodness or beauty, or utility, or happiness—practical ends. But science and philosophy are for truth, the theoretical end.

Bertha: O.K., I'm familiar with that distinction.

Socrates: But isn't it true that your three Western religions claim to teach the truth, not just make you happy?

Bertha: Yes.

Socrates: Then why do you ignore that aspect of them?

Bertha: How do I ignore it?

Socrates: Do you not say all religions are equal?

Bertha: Yes.

Socrates: But theoretical ideas are not equal. True ideas are not equal to false ideas.

Bertha: Oh, I see. Practical things are equal and relative, so they can be complementary, while theories are contradictory.

Socrates: Yes, but I do not think any religion would call itself a *theory*, a hypothesis. It's *theoretical* in the sense of aiming at truth, not just happiness.

Bertha: O.K.

Socrates: Now do you still say that all religions are equal?

Bertha: Yes.

Socrates: But you know how different their teachings are. So you must be ignoring or indifferent to their teaching aspect, and thinking only of their practical aspects. Is that true? Do you see teachings as unimportant? Is the business of religion something other than truth, do you think?

Bertha: I think it's something other than what *you* think of as truth, Socrates.

Socrates: Did my definition of truth not satisfy you?

Bertha: No.

Socrates: Why not?

Bertha: There's a far deeper truth, a higher truth, a more mysterious truth than you know about.

Socrates: Perhaps there is. But is there not also the truth I do know about, this ordinary, humdrum, common-sense kind of truth—saying what is?

Bertha: I guess so, but why is that so important to you?

Socrates: Because without it, how can one say *what is* about anything, even this higher truth of yours? To tell the truth about your higher truth, you must speak my lower truth.

Bertha: O.K., so your truth exists, Socrates, but it's not the essence of religion. All right, I know your next question, Socrates, you needn't even say it. I know how your mind works by now.

Socrates: Well? I'm waiting.

Bertha: What *is* the essence of religion? Well, like any essence, it must be what all have in common, the universal element in all religions, the lowest common denominator, or highest common factor. It's religion itself. There's an answer you're bound to like. The essence of religion is religion itself.

Socrates: I am still waiting for you to tell me what that is.

Bertha: Oh, that can't be done in such a simplistic, abstract, a priori way.

Socrates: Then let's do it in a complex, concrete, a posteriori way.

Bertha: How?

Socrates: Let's begin, not with the common essence, but with the examples.

Bertha: All right.

Socrates: Is this essence of religion broad enough to include the religion of Buddhism? Buddhism is a religion, isn't it?

Bertha: Certainly.

Socrates: And Confucianism?

Bertha: Yes.

Socrates: But Buddhism and Confucianism do not believe in a God. They never speak of God. Isn't that true?

Bertha: Yes.

Socrates: Then this cannot be the essence of religion, belief in a God, or the worship of God, or the love of God, or faith in God?

Bertha: That's right. Religion isn't only worshiping God. It's any ultimate concern, any absolute value, any Greatest Good or ultimate purpose to life.

Socrates: We now seem to have the thing you said you could not supply before—a definition. Let us test it. My disciple Plato did not believe in the gods, but he certainly believed in absolute values, a Greatest Good, and an ultimate concern and purpose to life. Would you call Platonism a religion?

Bertha: I guess the argument compels me to. But no, Platonism is a philosophy, not a religion.

Socrates: And what about these strange philosophies I have heard about that have caused so many wars in your century—fascism and communism—are they religions?

Bertha: No, they're antireligious. Communism is atheistic.

Socrates: But are they not ultimate concerns and purposes in life to their believers?

Bertha: Yes, they are that.

Socrates: Then the essence of religion cannot be any of these things, anything broad enough to include irreligion as well as religion. For how could a thing include its own opposite? How could religion include irreligion?

Bertha: People can be religious about their irreligion.

Socrates: That sounds like a contradiction. But perhaps it isn't. What do you mean by "being religious about it"?

Bertha: Being fanatical.

Socrates: So the essence of religion then is fanaticism? Only fanatics are religious?

Bertha: No, no, that's far too narrow. Not fanaticism, passion. Fanaticism is bad passion. Religious passion can be good passion.

Socrates: So the essence of religion is passion?

Bertha: Yes.

Socrates: Is lechery religion?

Bertha: In a sense, it is!

Socrates: I think I begin to see what this "sense" of yours is. You mean by "religion" a kind of attitude, don't you? Not a belief or teaching that claims to be true, but a quality of feeling, isn't that it?

Bertha: I guess that's it.

Socrates: But your three Western religions do not mean that by *religion,* do they? They all give you *books* that claim to teach you the very words of God, divine truth, divine revelation. It is only Eastern religions that mean by *religion* a certain state of feeling, or experience, or consciousness, isn't that right?

Bertha: Yes.

Socrates: So you are a Hindu or Buddhist or Taoist rather than a Christian.

Bertha: I don't know what I am, Socrates.

Socrates: Oh, neither do I. But I had thought you knew what you believed, at least.

Bertha: I guess I can't define the essence of religion broadly enough to include Buddhism and narrowly enough to exclude communism.

Socrates: Perhaps that is not your fault. Perhaps no one can define this essence, this lowest common denominator, for a very good reason. Perhaps it does not exist.

Bertha: Oh, but it does, Socrates. You can see it reflected in the different religions of the world. If you compare Jesus' Sermon on the Mount and Buddha's *Dhammapada* and Lao Tzu's *Tao Te Ching*

and the *Analects* of Confucius and the Proverbs of Solomon and
the Law of Moses and the *Bhagavad-Gita* and the Dialogs of Plato,
you see a striking oneness. Yes, Socrates, I see you with your
mouth open again, about to ask the obvious question, What *is*
that oneness? Well, look here. I think I can show you something
very striking. There are three different levels of insight in the
world about how to live. Most people live on the lowest level by
instinct and selfishness and pragmatism. And there are some
philosophers, like Machiavelli and Hobbes and Freud, who even
justify this and say it's as high as anyone can ever go, because
we're just basically animals. Then some people go higher and live
by justice and fairness and objective rightness and virtue. They
live by what ought to be rather than by what they want or feel
like. And most philosophers justify this way of life—Plato, for
instance. It's justice. Finally, a very few people live by something
even higher—charity, self-giving, going beyond justice. And the
thinkers I just mentioned write about that. They reach the third
level. That's the essence of religion. There it is, if you want a
teaching, Socrates—the teaching common to Moses, Solomon,
Jesus, Buddha, Confucius and Lao Tzu: die to self, mystical charity. I think even Plato reached that, didn't he? In fact, I'll bet you
had a hand in that. You must understand what I'm talking about.
Don't you?

Socrates: I understand indeed, Bertha, and I did have a hand in
Plato's philosophy. But this is still philosophy, not religion. It is
that division of philosophy called ethics, and that part of ethics
that deals with the question of the *summum bonum*, or greatest
good. So it's ethics. A way of life.

Bertha: All right.

Socrates: Then the essence of religion is ethics.

Bertha: If you like.

Socrates: No, if *you* like.

Bertha: Yes, I like. I say so.

Socrates: And you say that religion is this third level?

Bertha: Yes.

Socrates: And that not everyone reaches it, or understands it, or believes it?

Bertha: Right.

Socrates: So not everyone is religious, then.

Bertha: Not in that sense.

Socrates: An atheist is not a religious believer, is he?

Bertha: No.

Socrates: Are all atheists wicked people?

Bertha: Certainly not. I know some atheists who are more trustworthy than most Christians I know.

Socrates: Then an atheist can be very ethical?

Bertha: Yes.

Socrates: Unselfish?

Bertha: Yes.

Socrates: Then the essence of religion cannot be ethics, if atheists can be ethical but not religious.

Bertha: Oh. That is illogical, isn't it?

Socrates: So we are back where we began. What is this essence of religion, then?

Bertha: I don't know, Socrates.

Socrates: Now we are making progress!

Bertha: But I do know that whatever it is, religions are equal.

Socrates: How easily we abandon our progress! How quickly gravity pulls us down from the heights—or rather, how quickly pride's levity pulls us up from humility's gravity!

Bertha: But Socrates, don't you agree that religion is like a mountain with different roads to the top? That's why it's so hard to define—how can you define a mountain? Inside, it's all dark and mysterious and heavy. But the surface is visible, and you can see many roads on it, all leading to the top from different sides and starting points. How silly it is to fight about which road is best, which side is true! It's like arguing about whether the mountain is sunny or shady, hot or cold. It's both. It's all things. How narrow-minded to deny the validity of other roads than your own! Don't you see my point, Socrates? That's not pride, but humility. It would be pride to deny it, to absolutize your one way.

Socrates: I see nothing until I look. Let us look at what your mountain metaphor means. The various religions are the roads up the mountain of life to God, who is at the summit?

Bertha: Yes—God, or whatever you call him or her or it.

Socrates: The roads are equal because they all begin level, at the bottom, and they all reach the top?

Bertha: Yes.

Socrates: How do you know they all reach the top?

Bertha: How do you know they don't?

Socrates: I don't. Nor do I claim to know. But you seem to be claiming to know that they do. I wonder how you can know that, unless you stand at the top.

Bertha: No, I'm not at the top. I don't assume that.

Socrates: Here is something else you do assume, I think—that you know that all religions are manmade, that they are man's roads to God rather than God's road to man. That is how you think of religions, isn't it?

Bertha: Yes.

Socrates: I wonder how you know that. How do you know it isn't the other way round, as your own religion claims it is—your Scriptures, anyway—that it's God's search for man rather than man's search for God?

Bertha: I don't know. What difference does it make, really?

Socrates: If it is God's invention rather than ours—mind you, I do not know whether it is or not—then it would make sense that there be only one road, the one made by God. If, on the other hand, religion is manmade, then it is reasonable that there be many roads, for there are many men and nations and cultures. And if religion is manmade, it would be reasonable that all religions be fundamentally equal in being human, and finite, and mixtures of good and bad. But if religion is God-made, it would be reasonable that other religions, human religions, be unequal to the one God made, because human things are unequal to divine things.

Bertha: I never thought of it that way before.

Socrates: I think you did. You just didn't make your assumption explicit. That is all I do for you. I do not tell you what you do not know, just what you know but don't know you know.

Bertha: What assumption?

Socrates: You thought it arrogant to claim that only one religion is the truth, the whole truth, and nothing but the truth, because all human things are essentially equal. Wasn't that your argument?

Bertha: Yes.

Socrates: The conclusion follows from that premise only if you assume the other premise, that religion is a human thing. Your argument, then, was that manmade things are equal, and religion is a manmade thing, therefore religions are equal. Now I ask you how you know your second premise, that religion is manmade?

Bertha: I don't know. I just wanted to avoid arrogance.

Socrates: That is a good desire, certainly. But are good desires enough, without knowledge?

Bertha: What knowledge?

Socrates: The knowledge that you lacked, that led you into arrogance, clean contrary to your intention to avoid it.

Bertha: What? How?

Socrates: Your lack of knowledge of whether God or man made the road. For if God made the road, and made only one, then it is not arrogance but humility to accept this one road from God, to believe it, and it is not humility but arrogance to insist that your manmade roads are just as good as God's road. And is it not also arrogant to assume that you know that it is impossible that God made a road?

Bertha: I guess so.

Socrates: I think you are wiser than Professor Shift. He thought he was humble when he was arrogant. You, at least, admit you were arrogant, and that is humble.

Bertha: Shift did seem awfully sure the road couldn't be God-made.

Socrates: Perhaps that is why he stopped searching for it, sure that it could not exist.

Bertha: What do *you* think, Socrates?

Socrates: Me? Oh, I am still in search of such a way, though I do not know whether it exists or not.

Bertha: Is that why you're registered for Christology class?

Socrates: I'm not sure.

Bertha: Come on, it's almost time for that class. We have to walk across campus. I'll show you the way.

Socrates: That is precisely what you are doing.

Bertha: While we walk, I have another question that's bothering me. Don't you agree with the principle "by their fruits you shall know them"?

Socrates: It sounds like the principle of reasoning from the effect to the cause. Yes, I agree.

Bertha: Then can't you see that the fundamentalists can't be right because of the terrible consequences of believing what they believe?

Socrates: What terrible consequences?

Bertha: Religious imperialism, domination, my way over your way, my way is the only way, I'm right and you're all wrong—you know the attitude I mean.

Socrates: I do indeed, but I do not see how one who believes that a certain religion was revealed by God must take such an attitude. He would believe his religion not because it was his, but because it was God's, not because he made it up or wants to condemn others, but because God revealed it, wouldn't he?

Bertha: He *should*, anyway.

Socrates: And then it would be humility and not arrogance to be faithful to what God had said, and arrogance and not humility to revise it, wouldn't it?

Bertha: Yes, as before.

Socrates: We have a hidden assumption again, I think, in your worry about imperialism—that we can make religion whatever we want, that religion is manmade, as before. And I still do not know how you can know that.

Bertha: But there are a lot of Christians who *are* imperialistic and arrogant!

Socrates: This religion of yours, now, Christianity—it was taught by Christ, wasn't it?

Bertha: Yes.

Socrates: Was Christ an arrogant and imperialistic sort of person?

Bertha: Oh, no. Just the opposite. Nothing got him madder than the arrogance and bigotry of religious leaders. No man in history was ever more merciful and meek and compassionate to everyone.

Socrates: And did he teach that his religion was the one and only way?

Bertha: Actually, according to the texts, yes. He claimed to be "the way, the truth, and the life."

Socrates: That surely sounds like an arrogant claim.

Bertha: Yes. That's why I have to doubt that the texts are historically accurate. There's no way I can reconcile the two sets of texts, the humble ones and the arrogant ones.

Socrates: I hope we shall learn more about this matter in our Christology class. What you say seems to be true . . . unless, of course—but no, that's too fantastic.

Bertha: What's that?

Socrates: Arrogance means claiming more for yourself than is true, doesn't it?

Bertha: Yes.

Socrates: If any man claimed that he or his road was the only truth, the only way, it would be claiming more than a man has a right to claim in truth, would it not?

Bertha: Exactly.

Socrates: And thus it would be arrogant.

Bertha: Yes. You're beginning to see my point, Socrates.

Socrates: But if a god spoke those words—no, the thought is too fantastic to follow up, and it should wait until our next class, at any rate. Are we almost there?

Bertha: I think *you* are, anyway. [*They walk on.*]

Socrates: Hmmm. Tell me, how long has this religion of yours been around?

Bertha: About two thousand years.

Socrates: Remarkable! And have you Christians consistently followed your teacher in being compassionate like him?

Bertha: Alas, no, Socrates. There was even a time when some Christian leaders burned to death heretics, people who didn't believe as they did. That was called the Inquisition.

Socrates: What an astonishing contradiction!

Bertha: Yes. Now you should understand why people like Professor Shift fear fundamentalism. He wants to steer far away from anything like that.

Socrates: Do fundamentalists want to burn heretics?

Bertha: No, but they don't value religious tolerance or equality as liberals do.

Socrates: This Inquisition failed to distinguish the heresy from the heretic, it seems.

Bertha: How do you mean?

Socrates: They tried to destroy the heresy by burning the heretic, isn't that it?

Bertha: Yes. Wasn't that a stupid mistake?

Socrates: Indeed. Yet I wonder whether your compassionate professor is not making the same mistake.

Bertha: [*profoundly shocked, stopping in her tracks*]: What? How can you say that?

Socrates: He wants to love and embrace and tolerate all men as equal, does he not?

Bertha: Exactly. So how can you say he's like the Inquisition?

Socrates: I did not say that. I said he may be making the same mistake as they did in failing to distinguish the heresy and the heretic.

Bertha: How?

Socrates: Would you agree that heretics deserve acceptance and love and compassion, like all men?

Bertha: Of course.

Socrates: And what about heresies? Errors? Falsehoods? Do they deserve acceptance or rejection? Do we do good to ourselves and to others by believing falsehoods, or by rejecting them?

Bertha: Do you mean you think Shift is a heretic?

Socrates: No. I think he's afraid to disagree with anyone except a fundamentalist, or to call any religious idea heretical or false, because he's treating heresies as if they were heretics, just as the Inquisition treated heretics as if they were heresies.

Bertha: But he doesn't like to put anyone down.

Socrates: Will he put any *idea* down?

Bertha: Only fundamentalism. He believes Christianity is the religion of love, only love.

Socrates: And not of truth also?

Bertha: Not truth without love, no.

Socrates: But of love without truth? How could that be true love? How can those two divine attributes be separated? Should we not always be speaking the truth in love?

Bertha: "Speaking the truth in love"—that's a quotation from St. Paul. Have you read the New Testament, then?

Socrates: Not yet.

Bertha: Then how did you know that quotation?

Socrates: I did not know it was a quotation. I knew it because it was a truth.

Bertha: [Surprised.] But I think all God ever expects of us is love and sincerity.

Socrates: How do you know what God expects?

Bertha: Well, what do you think God expects, if not that?

Socrates: I do not know. That is why I am here—to find out.

Bertha: Well, if I were God, that's all I'd demand.

Socrates: Need I point out . . .

Bertha: Yes, I know.

Socrates: Seriously, Bertha. Suppose sincerity were not enough?

Bertha: What else could be as important as sincerity?

Socrates: Truth. In every other area of our life we need truth, do we not?

Bertha: For instance?

Socrates: Is sincerity alone enough for a surgeon? An explorer? Don't we need true maps to find our way?

Bertha: That's where we have something outside us, like a body or a land, to deal with.

Socrates: Do you think that we have nothing outside us in religion to deal with? Do you think God is somewhere inside you only, and not outside? Or do you think that the only thing outside is matter?

Bertha: I guess I was assuming that.

Socrates: And so you were assuming materialism, and therefore atheism.

Bertha: But religion is different from surgery or exploring.

Socrates: I wonder. Is it not a kind of surgery of the soul, and an exploration into God?

Bertha: It's a matter of the spirit, not the body.

Socrates: Indeed. But does not the spirit have roads that are just as objective as the roads of the body?

Bertha: What do you mean?

Socrates: Just as two different bodily roads lead to two different cities, and two different logical roads lead to two different conclusions, so two different spiritual roads lead to two different destinations: to God, or not to God. If, of course, God is really there. You aren't an atheist, are you?

Bertha: No, but I still think sincerity and honesty is the most important thing. I'd rather be sincerely wrong than insincerely right. Wouldn't you?

Socrates: Not if I were a surgeon or an explorer, no! It seems to me that true sincerity wants to know the truth, and true honesty wants to believe a thing for one reason only—because it is true. Do you disagree with that?

Bertha: But if that's so, then do sincere but mistaken pagans never go to heaven, never find God?

Socrates: I do not know that. I think you have before you such a case, of a sincere but mistaken pagan who is *looking* to find God, at least. I do not think a just God would punish anyone for not knowing what they could not know, or for disobeying a knowledge they did not have. But a just God *would* hold everyone responsible for the knowledge everyone *can* have, and for disobeying that knowledge. That is the situation I seem to see myself in—and most men, I suppose. If I did not know the truth at least enough to know that I often sin against it, why would I be searching still?

Bertha: But Socrates, I thought you were so good!

Socrates: Did you never hear the story of the Sophist physiognomist who tried to read my character through my face?

Bertha: No. Tell me.

Socrates: He came from another city, and knew neither my face nor my reputation, and boasted that he could read a man's character in his face. My disciples, more out of zeal than knowledge, were sure he would err with me, so they asked him to read my character. He stared at my face and pronounced me a lecher, a lazy lout and a bully. Everyone laughed but me, for they did not know me well, as you do not. I told them to stop laughing, and that the Sophist's art was no forgery, for those were precisely the temptations that I had to struggle against daily.

Bertha: Welcome to the human race, Socrates. But surely there's a little good in the worst of us, and a little bad in the best. There's good and bad everywhere, among people of every religion.

Socrates: Yes. And what follows from that?

Bertha: That all religions are equal—doesn't it?

Socrates: I do not see how.

Bertha: I—I guess I don't either, anymore. You confuse me, Socrates. What I thought I knew so simply and soundly turns out to be a cloud, and just dissipates away.

Socrates: Surely that is progress.

Bertha: It certainly doesn't feel like progress.

Socrates: If we build castles on clouds, they do not stand, do they?

Bertha: No.

Socrates: Would it not be progress, then, to abandon such cloudy foundations and to search for solider ones?

Bertha: Yes, I guess it would. So we have made progress, after all. At least we've made progress to our next class. Here we are. Professor Fesser's Christology class.

Socrates: Whom shall I meet here, I wonder?

7 Jesus: One of a Kind

Socrates and Bertha Broadmind stand in a crowded hallway in the Have It Divinity School, between classes.

Bertha Broadmind: Well, Socrates, are you ready for your first Christology class?

Socrates: I am always ready to learn.

Bertha: What do you hope to learn here?

Socrates: Two things, I think—who this Jesus person is and why divine providence brought me here to learn about him.

Bertha: Well, if anybody can teach you that, Professor Fesser should. He's a world-renowned expert in Christology.

Socrates: We are certainly at opposite ends of the hierarchy, then, because I hardly even know what Christology is. By the name, I take it that it is the science of Christ, the rational study of this Jesus person, who is called Christ?

Bertha: That's right. Hey! [*Entering classroom, seeing one round table with five students sitting around.]* It . . . It's going to be a seminar. You'll like that, Socrates. That means you get to ask a lot of questions.

Socrates: I should hope so. Is there any other way to learn? Aren't all of your classes like that?

Bertha: No, most are lectures.

Socrates [profoundly shocked]: Oh, I see. My method has not really caught on very well, then. And I suppose most of your reading is of books rather than of people.

Bertha: What do you mean by "reading people"?

Socrates: Dialog, of course.

Bertha: Oh. Well, we have that, too, but I guess we read mainly books here. What's wrong with books?

Socrates: Oh, nothing's wrong with them. They are a marvelous invention. But I do have two reservations about them.

Bertha: What?

Socrates: One of them I learned from the Egyptian legend about the god Thoth, who gave to the Pharaoh the invention of printing. The Pharaoh was unabashedly grateful, but Thoth warned that what he gave with one hand he took with another.

Bertha: What does that mean?

Socrates: That when we have a greater external memory, in a book, we have a lesser internal memory in the soul. That books can easily become like parasites, living off the blood of their host, the mind. And the second thing is that they are like corpses rather than like the living in that they always give the same answer back to you whenever you question them. I always preferred to dialog with the living, whose answers are unpredictable, rather than to dialog with the dead.

Bertha: Well, you'll get what you prefer here, all right. These characters all seem to be live ones. *[To the six other students, sitting down.]* Hi.

Students: Hi.

Professor Fesser [entering]: Good morning. Welcome to my seminar

in Christology. I am Professor Fesser, and I would like to hold
this class in as informal a way as possible, since I think we are
all advanced students and since we seem to have a nice small
group of—let's see—seven students, and since all of you are
very different, I think, and each of you has something unique
to contribute. I like to think of myself more as a facilitator than
as a lecturer. This is your class, not mine. So now that I've
introduced myself, I'd like to begin by having each of you in-
troduce yourself by telling us your name and something you
feel is important or useful for us to know about you, like why
you chose this course or why you're here at the Div School, or
where you're coming from, in general. O.K.?

Class: O.K. *[Some smile relaxedly, some seem suspicious.]*

Fesser: Let's start here at my right and go round the table.

Molly: My name is Molly Mooney, and I'm here to study the man
who is the unifying principle of the universe. Jesus taught us the
Way, the way of unity and love and oneness, and that's the secret
of life, as all the great thinkers knew. For instance . . .

Fesser: Excuse me, Molly, but I think we should keep the intro-
ductions short, all right? There will be plenty of time for everyone to . . . uh . . . contribute something more at length later.
O.K.?

Molly [smiling sweetly]: O.K.

Fesser [fussing]: I didn't mean to cut you off or put you down. Far
from it . . .

Molly [smiling]: It's O.K., Professor. I'm with you. I'm with everybody. I accept you. I accept everybody. I love everyone. You see,
I live from the Principle . . .

Fesser [patiently yet nervously]: Yes, thank you, Molly. May we hear
from the next person now?

Sophia (in a cultured East Indian British accent): I am Sophia Sikh, and
I think I'm here because I *don't* know where I'm coming from,
really. My mother was a Baptist, my father was a Sikh, and I was
raised by my uncle in Oxford, who is an atheist. While I was at

Oxford I experienced what my mother calls a fourfold fall from grace: I became an Episcopalian, then a Unitarian, then an atheist, and finally a sociologist. [*Class gasps with mock horror.*]

Fesser: What an interesting background!

Sophia: That's what everyone says. Frankly, I wish someone would say something else, something more interesting than "How interesting."

Fesser [*slightly blushing, slightly fussing*]: Well, Sophia, I think in a class as diverse as this one you're pretty well guaranteed to find something interesting. And I'm sure you have a lot to give as well as a lot to find.

Sophia: What do you mean by that, please?

Fesser: I mean I'm sure you have a lot to teach the others as well as a lot to learn from them.

Sophia: Why are you sure of that, professor? You don't know me.

Fesser: Why, everyone has something to contribute, Sophia, no matter who they are.

Sophia: Isn't that what they say to stupid people but never to smart people?

Fesser [*surprised*]: Why, no, why do you say that?

Sophia: Did anyone ever say that to Einstein?

Fesser [*smiling, shuffling*]: I see. I suppose not. I'm sorry, I didn't mean it that way at all, Sophia.

Sophia: Oh, I didn't mean to make you feel uncomfortable, Professor. People often tell me I'm too frank for my own good sometimes.

Fesser: Oh, please don't feel repressed here. Say whatever you please, whatever's on your mind. This is an open classroom. That's the one rule I'd like to insist on—that we don't feel it necessary to bind ourselves by any rules. O.K.?

Sophia: Just as you say, Professor.

Fesser: Next, please?

Thomas: My name is Thomas Keptic. I'm a professional chess player, and therefore a pauper, even though my rating is 2400.

I used to be a Christian, I think, then I became a Marxist, and now I'm disillusioned with both and with everything else I've seen. I used to design software for computerized philosophy courses, but I got bored with that. I spent last year at the Institute for Advanced Studies, trying to computerize the application of Goedel's Proof to the belief-structure of each of the world's major religions. I'm here to see whether it might be possible to do the same with different Christologies within Christianity, like infrastructures on a universal value-free consistency grid.

Fesser: What an interesting approach! *[Sophia turns sharply to him, and he quickly smiles his little, embarrassed smile.]* I mean, that may well be a fruitful new approach to the Christ event. I look forward to hearing more from you and your . . . ah . . . your angle. Next, please?

Solomon [slowly, softly]: My name is Solomon Etude. I'm just here to listen, to think, and to learn.

Fesser: Is that all you want to say?

Solomon: Yes, I think that's quite enough for now. When I have something worth saying, I'll say it.

Fesser: Thank you, Solomon. Next?

Ahmen: My name is Ahmen Ali Louiea. I came here to get a degree so that I can become an ordained missionary to my people to teach them about Jesus the Savior.

Fesser: Thank you, Ahmen. There are many different approaches to the Christ event, you know.

Ahmen: You mean to the Savior.

Fesser: Yes, but the name you use carries a big bit of interpretative baggage, I hope you realize.

Ahmen: And your "Christ event" doesn't?

Fesser: It's meant to be neutral.

Ahmen: But "Christ event" isn't his name; it's your invention. And "Jesus" isn't my invention; it's his name.

Fesser: Ah . . . well, we can discuss the hermeneutical-heuristic-linguistic problem some other time. *[Socrates frowns.]* Ah, who is our next student, please?

Bertha: I'm Bertha Broadmind, and I'm here to study Jesus because he's one of my all-time heroes of liberality and love.

Fesser: Thank you, Bertha. And last but not least, who are you, sir, and why are you here?

Socrates: My name is Socrates, and I am here because the divine providence arranged it, for what ultimate end I do not know. *[Class smiles tolerantly.]*

Fesser: I see. Hmmm . . . perhaps some role playing would be a good device. Would you like us to call you Socrates?

Socrates: Indeed I would. I have always had a strong penchant for calling things by their proper names. *[Class laughs softly.]*

Fesser: Fine. I think you make up a wonderfully diverse group, and I hope each of you contributes to this seminar. Now I think we should design this course as we go along rather than having me impose some rigid schema of my own on it. What do you think of that idea?

Thomas: What if that's not what we want? Wouldn't you be imposing your rigid scheme of nonrigidity on us then?

Fesser [surprised, confused]: Do the rest of you feel that way too? *[A few shake their heads no.]*

Thomas: It's not a question of feeling, Professor. It's a question of logic and consistency.

Bertha: I like the open idea.

Molly: Me too.

Ahmen: But we can't just talk about *anything*.

Fesser: I think our only necessary agenda is that we focus on the Christ event.

Ahmen: What do you mean by that, please?

Fesser: Oh, just that we cover the basic topics of Christology, such as *Heilsgeschichte*, high Christology versus low Christology, demythologizing, resurrection faith, hermeneutics . . . *[Sees Socrates' hand up.]* Yes, Socrates?

Socrates: May I ask for some definitions of terms?

Fesser: Certainly. Just what we'd expect from you. But I also expected that students at your graduate level had already acquired a basic familiarity with these concepts.

Socrates: Perhaps I do not belong here, then.

Fesser: What courses have you had?

Socrates: None but life itself. You see, I died many years before those concepts were invented.

Fesser: Oh, yes, I see. Well, now, that might just be a very useful rubric for us to follow. How would we explain the Christ event to a man who died in 399 B.C., some two thousand plus years ago? Let's see, from 399 B.C. to A.D. 1987, that makes . . . um . . . 2386 years later.

Socrates: Excuse me, please, but what do *B.C.* and *A.D.* mean?

Fesser: Oh, good! Socrates wouldn't have understood those concepts, would he?

Socrates: I don't understand why you speak in the subjunctive mood, but I *don't* understand those concepts. Would you please explain them to me?

Fesser: Well, class?

Bertha: *B.C.* means "Before Christ" and *A.D.* means "anno Domini," Latin for "in the year of our Lord," or after Christ.

Socrates: Christ is your Lord?

Bertha [embarrassed]: It's just an expression.

Socrates: Oh! So Christ *isn't* your Lord? *[Ahmen smiles, as does Thomas.]*

Bertha: That's not the point.

Ahmen: Are you sure?

Socrates: What I want to know is why you date all of history in relation to this man. You must regard him as the most important man in history, is that right?

Bertha: Yes.

Socrates: Why?

Fesser: An excellent question to begin with. I thank you for doing such a good job with this Socratic approach, sir.

Socrates: Thank you for the compliment, though it is hardly a compliment to congratulate a triangle on being triangular. But I would prefer an answer instead.

Fesser: Well, class?

Molly: Jesus taught us how to live. *[Gushes "live."]*

Socrates: Was he a philosopher, then?

Molly: Oh, yes.

Socrates: Tell me, how many great philosophers have there been in your world since my day?

Molly: Oh, hundreds. Dozens, anyway.

Socrates: So why was Jesus so much better than the others that you date all of history around him?

Molly: I just told you. He taught us how to live.

Socrates: All right, I think you can guess my next question then.

Molly: You mean, what did he teach?

Socrates: Yes.

Molly: Unity.

Bertha: Love.

Ahmen: Salvation.

Bertha: Liberation.

Thomas: Superstition!

Socrates: There seem to be as many Christs as there are Christians. Is there one thing you all agree on?

Bertha: Love.

Others: All right, love.

Bertha: That's our answer. He taught us the way of love.

Socrates: Yes . . . ?

Bertha: What do you mean, yes . . . ?

Socrates: I meant, surely there is something more than that?

Bertha: Something more than love? No, love is the greatest thing in the world.

Socrates: Of course it is. I was not asking for something greater than love. I was asking for some more wisdom than this. *[Sophia shakes her head yes.]* I assumed that everyone with even a little wisdom knew the greatness of love. Do your wise men usually preach the greatness of hate? Do you have many philosophers who say, "Let's hear it for hate"?

Bertha: No . . .

Socrates: Then what makes this Jesus fellow different from other teachers of love?

Bertha: He was more radical than anyone. *[Others nod agreement, except Ahmen, Sophia and Thomas.]*

Socrates: In what way?

Bertha: In the way of love.

Socrates: I mean, in what way was he more radical?

Bertha: But I just told you. He was more radical about love.

Socrates: But I don't know what you mean by *radical.*

Bertha: Oh. Well, he taught that you should love even your enemies.

Socrates: So did I.

Molly: He was killed for his teaching.

Socrates: So was I.

Bertha: He had thousands of disciples.

Molly: He lived what he taught.

Socrates: So did I.

Bertha: He liberated people from ignorance and superstition and prejudice and sexism.

Socrates: So did I.

Bertha: He taught a high monotheism.

Socrates: So did I.

Molly: And an ethical idealism . . .

Socrates: So did I.

Molly: But he was cosmopolitan and universalistic and unificationary . . .

Socrates: So was I.

Bertha: He told people of life after death.

Socrates: So did I.

Molly: He was a prophet, a servant of God.

Socrates: So was I.

Bertha: Are you saying you're as great as him, then?

Socrates: No, no, on the contrary, I'm assuming just the opposite! How absurd to think all of history would be dated around me! No, I'm asking you *why* he was so much greater than me or anyone else.

Bertha: We told you.

Socrates: No you didn't. Everything you said so far applies to me too. How was he greater?

Thomas: Socrates, many people believe strange superstitions about him. They believe that he . . .

Socrates: But you, what do you believe? Please tell me what you believe before you tell me what others believe. I'm having enough trouble understanding the first thing without proceeding to the second.

Fesser: Good, good. Let's back up and see what we've found so far. Socrates, what have you learned from the class so far?

Socrates: They have told me two things: one, that Jesus was the greatest man in history and that is why years are dated around him, and two, that the reason for his greatness is that he taught a radical philosophy of love.

All: Right.

Socrates: But many others also taught this philosophy. What makes Jesus distinctive?

Bertha: Why does he have to be distinctive? Maybe we identify with him because he *wasn't* distinctive. He was everyperson. Not even everyman. The masculine pronoun is proof of the culture's chauvinism.

Socrates: Surely you can't mean that? Would it be chauvinistic to refer to me as *he* rather than *she*? Or do you insist on *it*?

Bertha: If Jesus was only a *he*, then only half the world can identify with him. Women are out.

Socrates: I don't know what you mean by "identify with him," but surely, if he existed, he must have been either a man or a woman. Or was he of a third sex that I do not know about?

Bertha: That's a sexist attitude, Socrates.

Socrates: Of course it is! It's a question about his sex. Am I forbidden to ask such a question? I don't understand.

Bertha: Jesus was not sexist.

Socrates: Do you mean he was not a man? Was he a woman?

Bertha: Not literally, not biologically, but . . .

Socrates: Was he a man then?

Bertha: Not at the expense of the female, no.

Socrates: Is Jesus an archetype, then? Is he Humanity-as-such, a myth, a symbol?

Bertha: I can feel comfortable with that, yes.

Socrates: I didn't ask about your feelings. I asked about the facts.

Bertha: What do you mean by that?

Socrates: I wasn't asking about you, I was asking about Jesus. Was Jesus an actual individual male human being on earth or not?

Bertha: Well, yes, of course, but he was a very different kind of man.

Socrates: Good. Now how was he different?

Bertha: He was androgynous, if you dare.

Socrates: Jesus was androgynous?

Bertha: Yes.

Socrates: You mean he had female sex organs as well as male?

Bertha: No, androgynous in a spiritual sense, not a physical sense.

Fesser: We seem to be getting off the track. Bertha, do you believe androgyny is the reason that the world dates its years around Jesus or not? That was the question we started with, after all, and have not yet answered.

Socrates [surprised and pleased]: Why, thank you, Professor, for keeping us on target. I eagerly await your answer, Bertha.

Thomas: Of course that's not the reason, Socrates.

Socrates: Then why *do* you date your history around him?

Thomas: It's just a custom.

Socrates: Does the custom have a reasonable basis?

Thomas: Define "reasonable basis."

Socrates: Does Jesus deserve such special attention?

Thomas: I don't think so.

Molly: Well, I do.

Socrates: Why, Molly?

Molly [realizing she overstepped herself]: Uh . . . well . . . I'm not sure.

Socrates: Then perhaps it is time now to turn from what *you* believe about him to what others believe, which I resisted doing earlier.

Bertha: You mean perhaps others will give you a better answer?

Socrates: Yes.

Thomas [blurts out]: People say he was God.

Socrates [thinking he heard wrong]: Excuse me?

Thomas: Many people believe he was God.

Socrates: A god, you mean.

Thomas: No, *the* God, the supreme God. The one and only God.

Socrates: Evidently you mean by the word *god* something very different from what I do, especially when used in the singular.

Thomas: No, Socrates. If anything, the God they talk about is even more divine, or more exalted, or more perfect than the God you talk about.

Socrates: And they say that Jesus the man, the human being, was this supreme God?

Thomas: That's what they say, yes.

Socrates: Who? Who believes this . . . this thing?

Thomas: Christians.

Socrates: All Christians?

Thomas: Many of them, anyway.

Socrates: The majority?

Thomas: I think so.

Socrates: Is this a recent view? Are Christians of this sort a small sect?

Thomas: No, it's the traditional view.

Socrates: For how long?

Thomas: Ever since Jesus lived.

Socrates: Remarkable! Well, to turn from quantity to quality, what about your philosophers and theologians? Do the wisest among you believe this?

Thomas: Until recently, most Christian philosophers and theologians did.

Socrates: Even more remarkable! And what about your holy men and holy women?

Thomas: The saints? They're even more unanimous.

Socrates: Is this the official teaching?

Thomas: Yes. All the creeds teach it.

Socrates: Creeds?

Thomas: The official statements of belief.

Socrates: There are more than one?

Thomas: Yes.

Socrates: And they all say this?

Thomas: Yes, in different ways.

Socrates: And what about Jesus' immediate disciples, those who knew him personally? Did they believe he was God?

Thomas: Yes. You see, Socrates, a superstition is very powerful once it gets started . . .

Socrates: So it seems. And who did start it?

Thomas: Well, according to the records, he did. That's why they crucified him—for blasphemy.

Socrates: He himself claimed to be God?

Thomas: Yes.

Socrates: He actually said this?

Thomas: Yes, according to the only records we have, the four Gospels.

Socrates: On one occasion only?

Thomas: No, many times, in many ways.

Socrates: How? In what ways?

Thomas: He called himself the Son of God. He claimed to be sinless and to forgive the sins of the whole world. He said he would come at the end of time to judge the whole world. He said things like "I and the Father are one" and "He who has seen me has seen the Father" and "Before Abraham was, I AM."

Socrates: You do not believe this, do you, Thomas?

Thomas: No, Socrates, it is clearly irrational.

Socrates: So it seems. And you others, what do you believe about this Jesus fellow?

Bertha: [*looking disparagingly toward Thomas*]. More than *he* does, anyway.

Socrates: Do you believe he was *God?*

Bertha: No.

Sophia: I don't think so.

Socrates: Why do you study him then?

Bertha: He was a great philosopher, a wise man.

Socrates: Oh, no, that, at least, cannot be.

Bertha [*surprised, as all others also suddenly look up*]: What? Why not?

Socrates: I think I can show you that very easily. Thomas, do you think he was a great philosopher? What do you believe about him?

Thomas: I don't believe anything. I certainly don't believe he was God.

Socrates: Do you believe he was a great philosopher?

Thomas: No. I believe he was a great fake. I think he started the world's greatest superstition.

Socrates: Thank you. Do any of you believe he was God?

Ahmen: I do.

Socrates: I see. Then only you, Ahmen, have the right to believe that he was a great philosopher.

Others: What? Why?

Socrates: Why, it's very simple. The man claimed to be God. If he is, then only Ahmen is right. But if he isn't, then only Thomas is right. Because a mere man who claims to be God cannot be a wise man. In fact, he seems to be quite seriously insane. So whether he is or isn't who he claims to be, only one of you could possibly be right, and the majority of you must be wrong in either case.

Bertha: But he certainly *was* a wise man. Read the Gospels and you'll see that.

Socrates: That is not possible.

Bertha: How do you know? You never read them.

Socrates: Don't you see? It cannot be, any more than a triangle can have four sides. A mere man who claims to be God cannot be a wise man, and a God who claims to be God is not a mere wise man either. The first is a fool and the second is God. Jesus must be either a fool or God. The only thing he could not possibly be is a mere wise man.

Bertha: Then why do many people think that's just what he was?

Socrates: My question precisely. And I ask it now not of many people, who are not here, but of you who are. Why do you select the most illogical possibility, the only one that is inherently self-contradictory? Surely you know logic?

Bertha: Professor, can you help me out?

Fesser: I'm not sure that's my proper function here.

Socrates: Oh, I would be very grateful if you would, Professor. It would help *me* out. Surely you agree with my reasoning?

Fesser: I can't say I do, Socrates.

Socrates: Do you see any error in the reasoning?

Fesser: It's not that.

Socrates: Surely you do not believe this man was God?

Fesser: No, not in the sense I think you mean it, of course not. But you seem a bit rigid and overlogical to me, Socrates, a bit simple-minded. Just like the historical Socrates.

Socrates: There is good reason for that, surely. A thing usually seems like itself. *[Class laughs softly.]*

Thomas: I disagree with you, Professor. I don't see how you can be too logical. Do you want us to make a few logical mistakes now and then? Do you want us to be illogical two per cent of the time—say, only when thinking about Jesus?

Fesser: No.

Socrates: Don't you all see that this man must have been insane?

Thomas: Socrates, they're all victimized by their culture's number one superstition. They don't dare to question it. *[Addresses them.]* You know, you're all madder than a madman to respect a madman so much that you date your history by him.

Fesser: It's just not that black and white, Thomas. Jesus could have meant many different things by his claims to divinity—if, indeed, it was he who claimed it.

Sophia: Perhaps it was someone else by the same name?

Fesser: That's not what I meant, of course . . .

Socrates: But what did *he* mean? Surely that must be the first question. What did he mean by *God?*

Fesser: Excellent question. Let's explore that one for next time. The time is nearly over. What did Jesus mean by *God?*

Thomas: That's easy. He was a Jew talking to Jews. He meant the God of the Jews, Jehovah, or Yahweh. He meant the God of his culture. All our concepts are conditioned by our culture, except logic and mathematics. That's why we need them, to rise above our particular culture and conditioning to the universal.

Socrates: Do you think there are no higher universals than those of logic and mathematics?

Fesser: Let's not get off on that tangent, please. The question is, What did Jesus mean by *God?*

Socrates: In other words, what kind of God was the God of the Jews?

Fesser: Yes.

Thomas: You have to read their Scriptures to find the answer to that question, don't you?

Socrates: Then let's do just that.

Fesser: Good. Here's what I propose. Let's follow up the line of investigation opened by our friend Socrates here and explore the Jewish background of Jesus, the Jewish concept of God, and also

the Jewish concept of God's Messiah, the Promised One, who
Jesus also claimed to be.

Socrates: This is getting more complicated.

Fesser: Here is a reading list on the subject. *[Passes out papers. Class
buzzes with slight interest.]*

Socrates [reading the reading list]: But these are all recent books.

Fesser: Yes, the most up-to-date scholarship.

Socrates: But shouldn't we secure our foundation before erecting
our building? Shouldn't we gather our data before interpreting
it?

Fesser: What do you suggest, Socrates?

Socrates: I would like to read these Jewish Scriptures. I have never
done so, as you apparently have. I think this disadvantage of
mine may also be an advantage, if what Thomas says is true
about how hard it is to escape being conditioned by our culture.
I have no cultural conditioning in Christianity to overcome. And
I think my example could also be a kind of model for you:
Wouldn't it be an excellent experiment for *all* of us to read the
Jewish Scriptures as if for the first time, like me? Of course we
can't wholly overcome our prejudices or escape our conditioning,
but shouldn't we try to do so as much as possible, at least?

Fesser: I think that's an excellent suggestion. The class meets
again in one week. Why don't you each read what you think will
be useful, whether in my reading list or in the Hebrew Scriptures
or in both?

Socrates: Shouldn't we all read the whole of the Scriptures?

Fesser: That would be ideal, of course, but I don't think we have
the time for that.

Socrates: How much reading would it be? How long are they?

Fesser: You know, Socrates, you really act like you don't know.

Socrates: Of course I do; I don't.

Fesser: They're about two thousand pages.

Socrates: In one week? That's less than 300 pages a day. I shall
read it all, at any rate.

Fesser: Read what you will. Your assignment is to be prepared to discuss Jesus' Jewish background, and especially the Jewish concept of God, for next time. I'll see you all here again next week. Thank you all. And thank you, Socrates.

Socrates: It is I who must thank you, after thanking the God who sent me here to learn about him from you.

8 How Odd of God to Choose the Jews

The scene is Professor Fesser's Christology seminar at Have It Divinity School, the second class meeting. Socrates, Bertha Broadmind, Thomas Keptic, Molly Mooney, Ahmen Ali Louiea, and Solomon Etude sit around the table. Sophia Sikh is absent. Professor Fesser enters.

Fesser: Hello. Good to see most of you back again. Anybody know whether Sophia has dropped the course?

Ahmen: Sophia has mono, but she's going to try to stay in.

Fesser: Well! In any case, it's good to see the rest of you back. I'm sure you remember your assignment over the past week was to follow up on the suggestion of . . . uh . . . Socrates, here, and do some independent reading and research on Jesus' Jewish background, specifically on the Jewish concept of God. You were to read whatever sources you thought would be most helpful. I passed out a reading list for the rest of you, but Socrates announced that he intended to read only the whole of the Hebrew

Scriptures in one week. Isn't that right, Socrates?

Socrates: That is correct.

Fesser: Well, let's start with you, then. Did you finish the whole Old Testament?

Socrates: Yes.

Fesser: And what did you learn from your reading, Socrates? Tell us first what you were looking for and then whether you found it, please.

Socrates: I was looking for what Jesus meant when he used the term *God*.

Fesser: Good . . . perhaps we should review how that question came up.

Socrates: Well, we were all puzzled—I was, anyway—by Jesus' claim to *be* this God, somehow, whatever that could mean. So the following train of thought occurred to me, and it seemed reasonable to follow it: In order to understand Jesus' great influence on history, which was the question I began with, I had to understand Jesus, of course. And in order to understand Jesus I had to understand his concept of himself, who he claimed to be. And since he claimed to be the God of the Jews, I had to understand the Jewish concept of God. And in order to do that, I had to read the Jewish Scriptures. So I did.

Fesser: Good. And what did you find?

Socrates: A number of very surprising things. Would you really like to hear them?

Fesser: Certainly. Why not?

Socrates: They are all familiar to you, I think, but not to me. I ought to be learning, and you ought to be teaching, rather than vice versa, isn't that so? Are you sure you want to hear all these things that are so old to you, though they are new to me?

Fesser: Isn't part of the Socratic method a kind of role reversal between student and teacher, so that you learn by teaching and teach by learning? You've done such a fine job playing Socrates so far that I think you can continue today and be our teacher;

that is how you will learn. Right?

Socrates: I assure you, I am not playing; this is quite serious.

Class [except Bertha]: Right, Socrates *[patronizingly]*.

Socrates: But that does not matter, really. The God is good to have brought me to such an accommodating place with such accommodating people. But Professor, are you sure the other students agree to this procedure?

Fesser: Let's ask them. What do you say, class? Shall we all quiz Socrates today?

Class: Yeah, yeah.

Fesser: Then it's settled. Now tell us what you learned from the Hebrew Scriptures, Socrates.

Socrates: I read the whole thing—all the history and all the prophecies and all the stories—with a philosopher's end in mind—the concept of God. And I learned a number of astonishing things which my previous concepts of the God had not prepared me for.

Thomas: That's because we always look at things through the prejudices of our past, our own categories, conditioned by our society. You can't escape the color of your own eyeglasses.

Socrates: Surely you can, Thomas, when you take them off and look at them rather than through them?

Thomas: You can't do that. You can't really be objective.

Socrates: Why not?

Thomas: Because your thoughts are determined by your society.

Socrates: Oh, but Thomas, that opinion seems to be like a man sawing off the tree limb he is sitting on; it contradicts itself.

Thomas: How?

Socrates: If every thought is totally determined by your social conditioning and not by the way things really are, independent of your social conditioning, then that thought too is determined only by social opinion and not by the way things really are. So it is no more likely to be true than its opposite—which you say it is. You see, it leaves no ground at all to stand on to do the very thing I think you want very much to do, Thomas, the thing I want to do too—to criticize and evaluate and understand our society. If we can never know how things really are, outside our society's conditioning process, then does it not follow that we can never criticize that conditioning and that society, and thus we become pure status quo conservatives.

Thomas: Not me, Socrates. No one has ever accused me of being a conservative.

Socrates: You must be either a conservative, or not a truth-teller, or illogical, Thomas. For if you tell the truth about your first belief, the one about conditioning, and if you are logical enough to draw the necessary consequence of that belief, then you must be a conservative. So take your choice. Which will you be? A teller of lies, a committer of fallacies, or a conservative?

Thomas: Now wait just a minute!

Socrates: Gladly.

Thomas: I'm a radical skeptic; that's what I am.

Socrates: If you are a radical, then you must have gotten your radical and antisocial ideas from some other source than your society and its traditions.

Thomas: Maybe I did get them from other sources.

Socrates: Yes?

Fesser: Excuse me, but I think we shouldn't move too far down this side road right now. It's a fascinating one, this question of determinism and social conditioning. But we do want to get back to our main question, which is Jesus' Jewish concept of God. We really don't have the time in this class to explore all these other questions in depth.

Socrates: Why not?

Fesser [surprised]: Why . . . because the classes are scheduled very tightly, of course.

Socrates: Do you mean that the pursuit of truth is conditioned by your social schedule?

Fesser: I guess you could put it that way, Socrates.

Socrates: I see. Thomas, perhaps you are a bit closer to the truth

than I thought. But let us return to our main question. I was
about to say that my old concept of the God was profoundly
shocked when I read these Scriptures of yours. For I found
there a concept of a God I had never met before, either in the
minds of my fellow Athenians, who believed in the gods the
state believed in, or in the minds of any who believed in other
gods, such as the Egyptians or the Orphics, or in my own mind.

Fesser: How would you contrast the Jewish God with the pagan
gods, Socrates?

Socrates: You use that word *pagan* in a rather loose sense, I think,
for the three concepts of God that I just mentioned are very
different. You also use the word as something of an insult, I
think, do you not?

Ahmen: I don't. Chesterton says that paganism was the biggest
thing in the world, and Christianity was bigger, and everything
else since then has been comparatively small. There's a summary
of the history of religion in one sentence for you.

Fesser [ignoring Ahmen]: Socrates, what was *your* concept of God?
And how was it the same and how was it different from the God
concepts of your contemporaries?

Socrates: Let's sort it out. The first and most important thing of
all, I think, is simply the belief that there are gods, or a god, of
some sort. This joins what you call paganism with all the other
religions of the world against atheism, or secularism, or human-
ism, or whatever you call your new minority view.

Thomas: It's not a minority view among most educated circles
today, Socrates.

Socrates: But of all the people who have ever lived, the vast majority have believed in some god.

Thomas: People of the past perhaps. But they're dead.

Socrates: Most people are, you know.

Thomas [surprised]: What?

Socrates: I only want to practice nondiscrimination to the dead.

Ahmen: Chesterton called that "the democracy of the dead." He

defined it as extending the franchise beyond the small and arrogant oligarchy of the living to include those who have been dis-
enfranchised not by accident of birth but by accident of death.

Fesser [annoyed by Chesterton]: We're getting detoured again. What
else can you tell us about your concept of God, Socrates?

Socrates: Well, in the second place, most people in my day thought
there were many gods, but strongly suspected that these were
all only many masks for the one God.

Molly: And what was this one God, Socrates?

Socrates: I would not name him.

Molly: Why not?

Socrates: Because I could not, in honesty.

Molly: That honesty cost you your life, didn't it, Socrates?

Socrates: How do you mean?

Molly: In Plato's *Apology*. If you had only said, "I believe in Zeus,"
or named any of the other gods of the state, they would have had
to let you go.

Socrates: That may well be so, Molly. I do not know how things
would have turned out, only how things did turn out. But I could never
claim to know what I did not know, especially about the God.
That would be impiety. For I believe my vocation to philosophize
was the God's doing.

Molly: The Delphic oracle, you mean?

Socrates: Yes. He seemed to select me out of all the Athenians and
even told my friend Chairephon that there was no one in the
whole world wiser than I, only because of my ignorance, or rather my knowledge of my ignorance. It is this that made me a
philosopher, together with my will to read the riddle of the oracle. It was my conviction that those who claimed to know the
most really knew the least, especially about the gods. But when
I tried to enlighten them about this, they began to hate me.

Thomas: Well, we don't hate you, Socrates. We're open-minded
here.

Socrates: Excellent! And what is your mind open to, Thomas? Is

it Truth? Do you think there *is* Truth and that it may come to
your mind some day? Is *that* the guest the door of your mind is
open to?

Thomas: Truth! You speak it with a capital *T*. That sounds like
dogmatism to me, Socrates.

Ahmen: Chesterton says an open mind is like an open mouth—
useful only if you have something solid to chomp down on.

Fesser: Could we move twenty-two centuries back from Chesterton to Socrates? What else did you think about God, Socrates?

Socrates: Another feature of my belief would be something fairly
close to Thomas's skepticism, I think: We do not really know the
nature or purposes of the God, though I hoped to find out. I was
a philosopher precisely because I was neither a dogmatist nor a
skeptic. For it is the business of the philosopher to inquire, and
to inquire we must believe both that truth exists and might be
known, and that we do not yet know it. The skeptic does not
believe in truth, or does not believe it can be known, while the
dogmatist does not believe that we lack it. Both of these, it
seemed to me, cannot be philosophers. But of the two I was far
closer to the skeptic than to the dogmatist when it came to the
knowledge of the God.

Fesser: All right, then, the existence, the oneness and the un-
knownness of God. What else, Socrates?

Socrates: Let us not be too hasty. Perhaps the nature of the God
is not *totally* unknown. For we do have some data from which we
may reasonably hope to derive some knowledge of the God—I
mean ourselves and our world. It seemed reasonable to me, as
to most men, to think that the God had something to do with
the shaping and designing of the world. If there is a divine providence, if things in the world are governed by the God, then
when we find the whole of the world showing forth certain
characteristics, it would seem reasonable to conclude that the
God has something like these characteristics, just as the artist
can be known from his art and the writer from his writings.

Fesser: And what characteristics did you find in the world that led you to conclude something about the nature of God?

Socrates: It was not what most people concluded. They saw this world as a mixture of good and evil, and that is why they concluded that the gods were a mixture of good and evil—either that there were some good gods and some evil gods, or that each god was partly good and partly evil.

Fesser: And you did not agree with that reasoning?

Socrates: No. My conviction, which Plato recorded in his *Republic*, was that the God had to be wholly good, that the true God was truly good and the source not of all things but of good things only.

Fesser: So you feel that people of your day were polytheists because of the problem of evil? They couldn't believe in a single all-powerful and all-good God because of the reality of evil?

Socrates: If you wish to put it that way. It certainly seems reasonable to think that if there were a single God who was both all-good (thus willing only good) and all-powerful (thus able to do all that he willed), it would follow that there would be no evil anywhere in the world, if indeed the whole world were presided over by this God.

Fesser: How did you account for evil, Socrates?

Socrates: There would seem to be only four possible ways: first, that the God is not all-powerful; second, that he does not care to rule this world; third, that he is not all-good; and fourth, that there is no God at all.

Fesser: And did you agree with any of these ideas?

Socrates: I suppose I thought of the God as something less than all-powerful. The idea of an all-powerful God never occurred to me, any more than it did to my fellow Athenians. Even when I conceived the notion that the God was one, I did not conceive the notion that the God created the world out of nothing. That was one of the surprises I found in the Jewish Scriptures. But we are getting ahead of our story. Before I tell you what surprised me in the Jewish concept of God, I am supposed to tell you what my previous concept was. And my answer to the problem of evil that you ask about was twofold: implicitly that the God was not all-powerful, and explicitly that evil was not a reality at all, but an illusion caused by our own ignorance.

Molly: That's right, ignorance is partial thinking. Truth is unity.

Ahmęn: Are you both saying that evil doesn't exist? That . . .

Fesser [quickly]: Let's not follow that side road now, all right? It's a big long one, the problem of evil. But we want to get to the end of two other roads first: Socrates' concept of God and the Jewish concept of God that Jesus had. Socrates, are there any other things you thought about God?

Socrates: I thought he had to have great wisdom and beauty, since we see both of these qualities mirrored so impressively in nature.

Fesser: Ah, yes. People of every age are impressed with that.

Socrates: But I think the people of your time have lost much of the strength of that sense.

Fesser: Why do you say that, Socrates?

Socrates: Are there any among you who are strongly tempted to worship the stars or the sun or the earth?

Fesser: Judaism and Christianity have put an end to that.

Socrates: But what has put an end to the *temptation* to do it?

Thomas: We are the demythologized generation, Socrates. We are wary of myth.

Socrates: It would seem that you no longer need demythologizing because you no longer have any more myths to *de*. Your continued wariness of myths seems like the fear of an extinct animal, or like the obsession of a man who keeps washing his hands after every speck of dirt is gone.

Thomas: Oh, but Socrates, people are still victimized by all sorts of superstitions and propaganda.

Socrates: Propaganda? Is that one of your myths? Let me guess. Is it the myth of the Proper Gander who refused to go on a wild goose chase after the beautiful bird of Truth?

Thomas: Bad guess, Socrates.

Fesser: And bad pun. I thought you were above that sort of thing.

Socrates: Aristophanes put me in a basket above the earth. It is a lie, I assure you. I can sink to even lower depths of verbal degradation. But back to the question—perhaps you have no nature myths because you have man myths instead. Perhaps your myths have only shifted from without to within. But I suppose that is another story, another side road, for another day.

Fesser: Yes. Is these anything else you want to add about God, Socrates?

Socrates: Not about the God but about what is owed to him. The people of my day usually believed that the piety owed to the God consisted in sacrifices and ceremonies, while I thought that the true sacrifice was to give up vice, and the true ceremony was a beautiful soul's activity. My society tended to separate what you would call religion and ethics, the God and the good. I tried to unite them. In fact, Plato called the supreme God simply "the Good." I thought the offering the God really wanted was not a perfect sheep but a perfect soul, so I identified piety with justice, or health of soul.

Fesser: Let's summarize the things Socrates concluded about God before he read the Jewish Scriptures. One, that God exists. Two, that God is one. Three, that God is largely unknown. Four, that God is all-good and therefore evil is an illusion. Five, that God has great wisdom and beauty, which are manifested in nature. Six, that what God wants is justice and perfection of soul. Is that about it, Socrates?

Socrates: It will do for now.

Fesser: Perhaps we should add one other thing. How did you come to these conclusions that were so different from those of your contemporaries, Socrates?

Socrates: By reason, of course.

Fesser: Then we should add this seventh point, that reason rather than tradition or myth is the way to know God. Correct?

Socrates: Yes. That is what I thought.

Fesser: Now what did you find about God in the Jewish Scriptures?

Socrates: Much in every way. Some of the things I found there I had already suspected. For instance, that there is only one God, and that he is perfectly good. Yet in connection with this, I was surprised at the vehemence with which it was forbidden to worship other gods. What I supposed to be a mere mistake of ignorance and innocence in multiplying the masks of God, was taken to be the worship of false gods, or even evil spirits, real demons. What I took to be confused gropings toward the true God, these books usually took to be rebellion away from him.

I also found that this one God was the God of the whole earth. Though this one people claimed to be the chosen ones—the only ones who truly knew him because he had spoken to them—yet their claim was that he was not the God of the Jews only but of all people. In that connection, it surprised me how your Scriptures somehow combined two different senses in which God is one: on the one hand, that there is only one true God and not many, so that God seems to be a particular; and on the other hand, that this God is universal, the God of all the earth, and that all goodness somehow resides in him. I had always thought that the only true universal was a quality rather than an entity— justice rather than Zeus, beauty rather than Aphrodite, truth rather than Apollo . . .

Fesser: Something abstract rather than concrete.

Socrates: Yes. I could never quite make up my mind which kind of oneness the true God had. I kept shifting between one kind of language and another, abstract and concrete. In your Scriptures I found a God who is concrete—not in the sense that he is material, of course, but in the sense that he is a particular, actual entity, a Somebody, with a definite nature, character and will. Yet this God is declared to be the God of all, as universal as any of Plato's forms.

I think the idea that enabled these books to speak of God as having both kinds of oneness, the oneness of a particular and the oneness of a universal, was the idea of creation, the idea that God created everything that exists except himself. It solves the following dilemma. On the one hand, if God is only a part of all-that-is, then he cannot be truly universal. On the other hand, if God is only the *whole* of all-that-is, then he cannot be particular. But here I met the idea that he is the *creator* of all-that-is.

And here is a second thing the doctrine of creation taught me. It explained how God could be all-powerful. No god who is only a part of the whole cosmos can have power over the whole. But the creator of the whole would have power over the whole, just as the teller of a story has power over the whole story.

Fesser: Didn't you find the idea of creation in your tradition?

Socrates: No. Our gods only shaped a world. They were parts of the cosmos, the ordered whole. The idea that God created the whole cosmos out of absolutely nothing is an idea I find simply staggering. I think that no one could have thought that up except by either insanity or divine revelation. I have still not decided which it is.

Fesser: What else did you find in the Jewish God?

Socrates: Righteousness. I always thought that the God is perfectly good. But this goodness of God seems to have a peculiar relationship to the goodness of the righteous deeds this God commands us to do. The connection seems to be: "Be ye holy for I the Lord your God am holy."

Fesser: What do you see as the importance of that point?

Socrates: That Euthyphro was wrong when he said that a thing is good only because the gods will it; rather, God wills it because it is good. I was right there, against Euthyphro. But I forgot to add, or rather failed to see that the reason a thing is good in itself, in turn, is because it somehow resembles God.

Fesser: Could you put that more simply?

Socrates: In other words, the nature of God as goodness is the foundation for the goodness of anything that shares in that nature to any degree.

Ahmen: I'm still not quite clear about that point, Socrates, and it's very important to me. Could you explain it again, please?

Socrates: Did you ever read the conversation Plato recorded that I had with Euthyphro?

Bertha: You mean you really had those conversations?

Socrates: Yes. Why is that surprising to you?

Bertha: Nearly all the scholars think they're mostly Plato's own invention.

Socrates: Hmph! Scholars! Do they think I am merely Plato's invention too? But it doesn't matter who speaks the truth, only that it is the truth that is spoken—except to a scholar, who is more concerned with the first thing than with the second. But let me try to explain my point to Ahmen a little more clearly. I asked Euthyphro the question: Is a thing good because the gods love it, or do the gods love it because it is good? Substitute God for *the gods* and you have the question I put to you now.

Ahmen, you believe this God described in your Scriptures really exists, do you not—a God who is all-good and wills only good?

Ahmen: Yes.

Socrates: My question to you, then, concerns the relationship between the will of this God of yours and the goodness of any deed. Do you say that a deed is good because God wills it?

Ahmen: Yes.

Socrates: Then your God seems arbitrary. Suppose he wills you to cut off your neighbor's ear tomorrow? Would that deed then be good?

Ahmen: If God willed it, yes—but . . . that does sound silly, doesn't it?

Socrates: The alternative, then, is that God wills the deed because it is good in itself.

Ahmen: That sounds better.

Socrates: Does it really? Would you have your God bowing down, so to speak, to a law higher than himself?

Ahmen: No. How would that follow?

Socrates: If the cause of God's willing a deed is outside himself, in the nature of the deed itself, then God conforms his will to the good of the deed, rather than determining the good of the deed by his will.

Fesser: Isn't that exactly what you taught, Socrates?

Socrates: It is. I was mistaken, it seems, for I could only conceive the one God on the model of the many gods, as the greatest and most perfect of the many, who had no need of the other gods, but still had need of a law outside himself. For the God of my conceivings did not create the cosmos, but was a part of it, and subject to its laws. But the God of your Scriptures is the lord of the cosmos and thus of its laws.

Fesser: Then you go back to the first alternative, don't you? That God's will is the sole source of goodness? Doesn't that make God arbitrary?

Socrates: No, because it is the nature of this God that is the cause and foundation of goodness—both the goodness of his will and the goodness of the deed.

Fesser: Oh. So you are saying, in other words, that God's will and the intrinsic goodness of certain deeds are not related to each other as efficient cause and effect, in either of the two possible ways: either, as Euthyphro thought, that the goodness of the deed is the effect of the will of God, or, as you thought, that the will of God is the effect of the goodness of the deed, but rather that both of these two things are effects of the same common cause, God's own nature. Is that what you say, Socrates?

Socrates: That is precisely what I say. I am glad to see that the conceptual tools of philosophers are so clear and so clearly used here at the academy.

Fesser [blushing]: It is a well-known solution to your dilemma, Socrates. Many of the great theologians of our tradition have taught it. Now what else did you find in the Scriptures that you did not know before?

Socrates: Another attribute of the Jewish God that is founded on the idea of creation, I think. I mean his omniscience, his all-wisdom. Your God makes no mistakes and has no ignorance about anything past, present or even future, because he seems to stand outside time, not in it. He does not wait, and he does not change. A thousand years are to him as a day, and a day as a thousand years.

Fesser: How does this contrast with the idea of God you had before?

Socrates: The only gods I and my society were able to conceive were only *somewhat* wiser than we, as we are somewhat wiser than infants. All they could do was to rule with their wisdom over larger portions of the cosmos than we can. But this God of yours rules the entire cosmos because he has wisdom for the whole, and he has wisdom for the whole because he designed and created the whole.

Fesser: I see. Interesting—I had not explicitly connected the doctrine of omniscience with the doctrine of creation before. Any other surprises, Socrates?

Socrates: The greatest of them is still to come.

Fesser: And what is that?

Socrates: What God wills, or rather his motive in willing. Let me try to explain. That God should have a will and a law for men came as no surprise to me, since the gods of my day had both. But that this supremely perfect God of yours, the God who, unlike the gods of my society, has absolutely no need of us, or of our worship, or of our obedience, or even of the very existence of the universe he created—that this God should nevertheless give laws for us and care so passionately that we obey them—this could have only one possible motive, and I found that motive constantly in your Scriptures, often implicit, sometimes explicit.

Fesser: What motive?

Socrates: If it is not for himself that he wills, since he needs noth-

ing, it must be for us that he wills. In other words, purely unselfish love, a kind of love I wonder whether it is possible for us
mortals to have at all, since we are creatures full of needs and
in time. We need at least a future; only a God who is not in time
and change does not.

Fesser: Yet the primary commandment is to love this God with
our whole heart and soul and mind and strength, and our neighbor as ourselves. You found that commandment in the Scriptures too, didn't you?

Socrates: Yes, and it is a great puzzle to me how we could possibly
obey it. If the love commanded there is unselfish love, how can
a self love unselfishly? How can a creature in time "be holy as
I the Lord your God am holy"? It seems to be an unsolvable
puzzle.

Fesser: Do you see a possible solution to it in the idea that we will
look at next, the claim in the New Testament that this God
became a man in Jesus?

Socrates: Oh! I see! How unthinkably wise! But how would we—
I mean, the God's power would suffice to assume humanity, but
surely human power would not suffice to assume divinity. So if
Jesus were this God who became a man, *he* would be able to
practice this divine love in time and history, but how could *we* do
it?

Fesser: I think we'll have to defer that question until next time,
after you have read the New Testament. Let's return to our topic
of the nature of the God of the Old Testament now, O.K.?

Socrates: Before we go on to do that, I must tell you that I had
the strangest feeling when I read these Scriptures of yours, especially when I came upon the strangest and most surprising
notions, like this one of unselfish love. What is so strange is that
these very strangenesses seemed somehow more natural, more
normal, more at the solid center of everything, than anything
else. It's difficult to explain. It's much more a certain sense, a
feeling, than anything I can define.

Let me put it this way. I had always instinctively groped after the true God, and I thought that if and when I found him, I would recognize him as something familiar. In a sense this happened to me as I discovered the God of the Jews, yet in another sense the opposite happened at the same time. I was shocked and surprised. My expectations were *not* fulfilled. And yet, in another and deeper sense, I think, they were. It felt as if something in myself that was wiser than I—my *daimon*, I think—which had always directed my search and had always known exactly where to move me to go and not to go—as if this *daimon* were showing me its own house.

Ahmen: That's it! Socrates, your *daimon* was the Holy Spirit!

Socrates: Who?

Fesser: Another topic that you will get to when you read the New Testament, Socrates.

Ahmen: The Holy Spirit is not a *topic!*

Fesser: Ahmen, in this class *everything* is a topic.

Ahmen: Then the Holy Spirit is not in this class.

Socrates: Excuse me, but if as you say I will get to this Holy Spirit when I read your New Testament, perhaps we should keep to one thing at a time now.

Fesser: Indeed we should. *[Slightly flustered.]* Now what were you saying, Socrates?

Socrates: That the occasion of reading your Jewish Scriptures was the most perfect example I ever encountered of one of my own most famous and important teachings, the doctrine of *anamnesis:* that all learning—that is, all learning of eternal truths—is really a remembering, a kind of bringing of unconscious knowledge to consciousness, as you would say. You could call it *deja vu*, or the "Aha!" experience. Like waking from a dream, or meeting a forgotten friend, or coming home to a place you had left so long ago that you had forgotten it, yet it was your own home.

Fesser: And this is how you felt about the Old Testament?

Socrates: No, about the God presented there.

Fesser: You were not puzzled by this God?

Socrates: Oh, yes, immensely. But the very puzzles and surprises often had that feel of home about them.

Fesser: Often? But not always?

Socrates: No, not always. For instance, I do not know what to make of the puzzle that this God of yours is eternal yet acts in time, in history. It makes sense that he act, for he is love, and love acts. But I thought love had to be a process in time. How could it be timeless? I did not think *thought* had to be a process in time, so I had conceived of God as pure thought. But how can a timeless God be pure love?

Ahmen: It's not like our love, Socrates.

Socrates: And how does that explain the puzzle of the timeless love acting in time?

Ahmen: It's got something to do with the Trinity.

Socrates: The what?

Fesser: No, let's not get into that yet. The real Socrates would certainly not be prepared for that, I think.

Socrates: If only a false Socrates would be prepared for it, does that mean it is a falsehood?

Fesser: No, let's just forget that for now. Socrates, can't you see how the unselfishness of God's love is connected with its time-lessness?

Socrates: I might, if I try. All this is so startlingly new to me . . . Let's see . . . Ah, yes, I think I see it. Human loves are temporal because they are based on need and desire to satisfy needs. Divine love is eternal because it is not based on need or desire. It is to desire what contemplation is to reasoning.

Ahmen: Could you explain that analogy, Socrates?

Socrates: Surely. Reasoning is a process aimed at finding the truth. Contemplation is the simple knowing of the truth already found. It need not be a process. Do you see that?

Ahmen: I think so.

Socrates: Similarly, desire is a process aimed at attaining the good,

its object. That is selfish love, love for the sake of yourself.
Unselfish love could be simply affirming the value of the other,
rejoicing in the good already present rather than seeking the
good absent. A timeless God could do this, I suppose.

Ahmen: I see.

Socrates: What still puzzles me is how a God who is changeless
could produce effects in time that are changing . . .

Fesser: I think that question is rather too philosophical and too
technical for us to go into it now, if you don't mind, Socrates.
Another interesting side road for another day.

Socrates: I hope I have many more days granted to me to explore
all those side roads we have exposed. But yes, let us get back to
the main road. I have not yet told you my greatest discovery of
all, my greatest surprise and my greatest puzzle in reading your
Scriptures.

All: What's that, Socrates?

Socrates: God's name.

Bertha: God's name? What's in a name?

Socrates: Everything. I think that things are in their true names.

Bertha: I don't understand. Names are just labels.

Socrates: I think not. Labels are only things. You think of names
as things. But I think of things as names. You think of names as
things in a world of things, things surrounded by other things.
I think of things as names, surrounded by true names. But this
is another side road. Let me try to explain my shock at the name
of God.

Fesser: There are many names for God in the Scriptures. Didn't
you already know of them from your own culture?

Socrates: I did. And those were all *our* names for him. I was not
surprised by the names the men in your Scriptures gave to God,
but by the name God gave to himself. All our names for him
really name not what he is in himself but only what he is in
relation to us . . .

Ahmen: Why is that so, Socrates?

Socrates: Look at the names: God, Lord, Creator, Lawgiver, Judge, Savior. He is not his own God, or creator, or savior, but ours.

Ahmen: I see.

Socrates: As I was saying, I found in your Scriptures something I found nowhere else and never even conceived: the true name of God, the name that expresses his own essential being, what he is in himself. At least that seems to be what he said when he spoke to Moses from the burning bush and called himself not only the relative name, "the God of Abraham, Isaac and Jacob," but also the absolute name, I AM, or I AM WHO I AM. That name seemed absolutely special.

Fesser: You're right, Socrates. That's the sacred Tetragrammaton, the name no Jew will ever pronounce. But what was the puzzle you found in it?

Socrates: *I* is the name for a subject of thinking or willing, is it not?

Fesser: Yes.

Socrates: What puzzles me is how we can study as an object the God whose very essence is to be subject? How can we even know this God at all? How can *we* be the *I*'s and turn God into our object, our *You* if by his own essential nature he is always *I*, always subject? We could never know him truly. Yet in saying his true name we *are* knowing him truly, it seems.

Fesser: A very sophisticated question, Socrates. How can we know I AM?

Ahmen: I think it's a very simple question.

Fesser: And you have a very simple answer, I suppose?

Ahmen: Yes! God speaks. We listen. Divine revelation.

Fesser: Socrates? Is that what you found there?

Socrates: Yes, it is. All the religions I had ever known had been man's search for God. This one seems to be the story of God's search for man. That is why I think the puzzle about how the God who inhabits eternity can search in the wilderness of time is an important one. If he had not done so, I do not see how we could have known him as he is.

Fesser: Why do you think no one else besides Moses could ever have come up with this notion of God?

Socrates: Did you not read the Scriptures? Moses did not come up with it; Moses came up to it. It was not Moses' idea; it was God's idea.

Fesser [a little annoyed, surprised and embarrassed all at once]: Oh . . . well . . . whether that is so or not, why do you think that neither you nor any other thinker ever would have come up with this idea, this name?

Socrates: Because I tried and failed all my life. Many nights I lay awake all night thinking about the problem of the true name and nature of the God, and all I ever came up with was my own ignorance.

Bertha: Plato didn't tell us about all those nights, Socrates. Why?

Socrates: I did not speak of them, even to him.

Bertha: Why?

Socrates: For three reasons. First, I did not wish to shake the faith of those who believed when I was not sure myself. Second, because this is a sacred mystery, which should not be the subject of public chatter. In fact I am quite surprised that my inner *daimon* has not forbidden me to speak of it with you. Third, because of the tendency of Plato and the young in general to dogmatize and systematize. I did not want to found a Socratic theology on my own ignorance.

Fesser: So what did you do?

Socrates: I thought and thought, dreamed and dreamed, prayed and prayed, that I might know the name of the God and the nature of the God—for the true name tells the nature—all to no avail. It was exactly like dashing up against a wall. I was an irresistible force, and it was an immovable object.

Fesser: So in this case the object won.

Socrates: Until now, yes. I could make no headway against the wind, it seemed. Now I know why. The wind came from God. I had to ride on it.

Fesser: I don't quite understand your metaphor.

Socrates: I had to simply listen, like Job, like Moses. I had to receive the truth as gift.

Fesser: And God did not give it to you?

Socrates: Not until now. He gave this secret to none of us Greeks. I do not know why. How odd of God to choose the Jews!

Ahmen: That's what Ewer said! Have you read him?

Socrates: No. When two men speak the truth, they need not be supposed to have copied from each other, but from the truth itself.

Molly: Now that's a really important question, I think. Did God really choose the Jews? How could the universal God be so provincial?

Fesser: Another interesting side road, Molly.

Socrates: See how severe we must be against ourselves and against our natural tendency to sit down at the side of the road, or to wander off into the fields to smell the flowers, if we want instead to get home! It seems we must ruthlessly oppose not only all ignorance but also ruthlessly oppose all knowledge if that knowledge leads us elsewhere than to the place we seek. How hard it is to keep our minds on one road at a time!

Bertha: Why do you think that is, Socrates?

Fesser: This is another side road, the very question of why it is hard to avoid side roads.

Socrates: Yes, but let me explore it briefly if I may. I strongly suspect that with God things are very different, and he can know everything at once. But we are not God. I think therefore that it is the desire to be God and perhaps the resentment at not being God that leads us to try to be like God and know all things at once.

Fesser: Interesting psychoanalysis, but I don't see why the I AM was so difficult for you to find or so startling when you found it. Could you explain that to us?

Socrates: I will try, though I shall have to use words as a potter uses clay. I could not see God as I AM because I could not see how I-ness and AM-ness could be one. I mean by I-ness and AM-ness personhood and perfection, and also subjectness and objectness, or the oneness of *someone* and the oneness of universal Being.

Fesser: That sounds like Sartre's dualism between being-for-itself and being-in-itself.

Socrates: I do not know this Sartre, but here is what I mean, at any rate. Take I-ness first. It is the mode of being of a subject, a knower and willer, a person. A person, at least a person with a will, would seem to be in time. Take now AM-ness—not *a* being but Pure Being Itself, eternal and unchangeable. This God must be unchangeable, because he is perfect. To change would be to acquire some new perfection or to lose some old perfection, or both. All three kinds of change are incompatible with absolute perfection—which, if I am not mistaken, this God is said to have. So it comes down to this: I could not understand how God could be in time and in eternity at the same time, if you'll pardon the expression.

Bertha: Please let's not go further down this side road. My head is splitting already with a time-and-eternity headache!

Fesser: I think it is not a side road, Bertha. Socrates, isn't it true that Plato sided with AM-ness and most of the people before him sided with I-ness? I mean, Plato substituted Justice for Zeus, and so with the other gods.

Socrates: Yes. Those seemed to be the only two options. I was not as quick as Plato to abandon the I-ness of the god, for it meant that though you could know the God, the God could not know you, or even if somehow he could, he could not love you, since I thought love was a process in time, and imperfect. I did not see how Eternal Being could love me. If the God loves me, then he is not eternal being. If the God is eternal being, then he or it cannot love me. How can Goodness Itself, or Being Itself, have a care, a will, a desire?

Bertha: And now you understand?

Socrates: Oh, no. I just see a glimmer of light on the horizon, a possibility. Perhaps to have it both ways. The God of your Scriptures is clearly eternal and perfect and unchanged by us, and universal. As the creator of time, he must be beyond time. But it is even more clear in your Scriptures that he loves, and cares and acts and speaks.

Bertha: Aren't we getting rather far afield from what was supposed to be our main point, Jesus?

Socrates: I think perhaps not. For such a God as I am beginning to grasp could even become a man if he wished.

Bertha: I don't see that. What's the connection?

Socrates: The unity of the I-ness and the AM-ness in God which allows him to work in time by giving a law and inspiring prophets and performing miracles, may also allow him to enter time bodily, to take up time into himself without losing his eternity, somehow . . . perhaps. I do not know whether this is so or not nor, certainly, *how* it is so if indeed it is. But the thing I thought of last week as utterly absurd and impossible, the idea that a human being named Jesus could be the supreme, eternal God who created the entire cosmos—this now seems possible, or possibly possible, or almost possible, or almost possibly possible.

Thomas: Wait, Socrates. I don't understand. You said that you discovered the transcendence, the distinctiveness of this Jewish God in their Scriptures—the ways this God transcends not only the imperfections of the pagan ideas of the gods but also transcends the entire universe by being its creator. I should think that this new notion of yours, the notion of God's transcendence, would make it much harder, not easier, for you to consider the possibility of an incarnation of this God. A God closer to nature could more easily become a part of nature, but a God so far removed from nature—how could he?

Socrates: I see your problem, Thomas, but I think it comes from thinking of spirit and the possibilities of spirit under the narrow

and confining laws of matter. It would be harder to go from
Egypt to Athens than to go from Sparta to Athens, therefore
it would be harder to go from heaven to earth than to go from
the sky to the earth. Isn't that it? But there are analogies even
in the material world for the truth I think I see: that transcendence makes immanence more possible, not less. Take light, for
instance. Light has no color. It transcends all colors. Isn't that
so?

Thomas: Yes. How . . . ?

Socrates: Isn't that precisely why it can be immanent in all color,
and not just in one? If light were yellow, it could not also be blue.
Because it is neither yellow nor blue, it can be both yellow and
blue. Or take thought, an even better example. It has no form.
It is not green, or square, or animal, or mineral. Isn't that so?

Thomas: Yes.

Socrates: And isn't that precisely why it can take upon itself all the
forms of the world, why it can know green, and blue, and square,
and triangle, and animal, and mineral?

Thomas: Common sense would say so. But I think science would
give another explanation. It's just cerebral biochemistry.

Socrates: Thought is just biochemistry?

Thomas: Yes.

Socrates: So the difference between a true thought and a false
thought is the difference between a thought with a large, or
small, or double electrical charge and one with another kind of
electrical charge?

Fesser: Another side road, gentlemen. Back to the main line,
please. We have only a few minutes left.

Socrates: How unnatural it feels to bow to Time, not just to Truth.
But it seems we must. All right, then, my point, Thomas, is that
God is more like thought than like things: Only a God who is not
a determinate part of the whole could enter into the whole from
outside, so to speak—another spatial metaphor—and become a
part of his own creation.

Thomas: Why must *outside* be metaphor?

Socrates: Why, because otherwise we could fly to him on wings, if we flew long enough.

Thomas [laughs]: But how could the God of the whole become only a part? Light is in *all* colors, and knowledge in *all* natural forms, but this God, according to Christians, became one specific human being.

Socrates: Perhaps it is like the author of a story putting himself into the story as one of his own characters, in due time, say in the third chapter. He would be both a part of the story, limited in space and time like any other character, and also outside the story and unlimited, the creator of the whole story.

Thomas: That would not be a miracle. The Incarnation is a miracle.

Socrates: Only to us, not to God. The author coming into his story is not a miracle to the author, but well within his natural powers. But it is a miracle to the other characters in the story.

Thomas: I see . . . so you would define a miracle as something like this, then—like an artist interjecting brush strokes into his painting that didn't follow the other strokes, or a musician interjecting notes into a symphony that didn't follow the progression of previous notes and couldn't be predicted by them?

Socrates: Something like that.

Fesser: Another side road, miracles. Gentlemen, the bell is about to ring. Let's finish up, please. Where do you think we should go from here, Socrates? Do you now think the Christ event is very likely, considering the nature of this God of the Jews?

Socrates: Oh, no, I did not say that. It would still be a profound shock. Did it not shock the Jews, according to your records?

Ahmen: I'll say it did!

Socrates: I thought we were considering only the nature of this God, not whether he did in fact become a man, or even whether it is possible for him to become a man—though that topic did come up when considering his nature—nor even whether such a God really exists or not. We were just exploring the concept, the essence.

Fesser: And what did this discovered essence teach you, Socrates, if you can sum up in one minute?

Socrates: I see it can be useful to be under time pressure and not at leisure. Hmmm! Well, two things, in sum. First, it made it possible, just barely possible, for me to entertain the possibility of this event you call the Incarnation of the God. Second, it taught me something of what Jesus must have meant when he used the word *God* and claimed to be this God.

Fesser: And where do we go from here, logically, Socrates?

Socrates: Into two things I think: first, whether in addition to being possible, the Incarnation is actual, and second, who this Jesus fellow was. For both reasons, I should like to read your New Testament now.

Fesser: An excellent suggestion and a logical progression, don't you agree, class?

Class: Yes.

Bertha: It's back to basics. The New Testament in Christology class! Wow!

Fesser: Well, I think the theologian should be scientific, and the good scientist always starts with his data, doesn't he? Let's all read the Gospels, at least, for next week. I have a reading list here too, for whoever wants it. *[Passes it out.]* Read whatever you think is useful for next time. We'll spend the next class discussing the two questions Socrates ended with. O.K.?

Class: O.K.

Fesser: I'm sorry we didn't get to hear more from the rest of you today, but I think Socrates here has summed up pretty well what a pagan would find in the Old Testament if he read it for the first time, don't you?

Class: Yeah. Nice going, Socrates. Great performance.

Fesser: Then it's time to move on. See you next week.

9 Look Out!
It's Alive!

The scene is the third class meeting of Professor Fesser's Christology course at Have It Divinity School. Socrates sits alert, thoughtful, silent and peaceful. Bertha, Molly, Ahmen, Solomon and Thomas are present, chatting. Sophia is absent.

Fesser *[entering, breezily]*: Well, well, everyone's here.

Bertha: No, Sophia's gone. She dropped the course.

Fesser: Oh, too bad. Well, let's plunge right in. We agreed to follow up on the suggestion of our friend Socrates *[smiles patronizingly at Socrates]* and review the New Testament texts this time, in light of our Old Testament readings last time. Socrates was going to try to read them as if for the very first time. I think that would be a fascinating experiment—to imagine what an ancient Greek philosopher would get out of the New Testament if he read it.

Socrates *[shaking his head slightly]*: It was not imagined. It was real.

Fesser: All right, then, Socrates, what did you get out of the New Testament?

Socrates: Far more than I bargained for.

Fesser: Tell us about it. What do you know now that you didn't know before?

Socrates: I know now why I was brought back to life in your time. It was to meet a person who was born four hundred years after I died.

Fesser: Jesus of Nazareth, of course.

Socrates: Yes.

Fesser: And you met the real Jesus, just as we are meeting the real Socrates?

Socrates: I did.

Fesser: I think it's remarkable what a little bit of psychodrama can effect. A bit of well-played pretense can really be instructive.

Socrates: I think it's even more remarkable what a real, live person can effect. I am no pretense, and neither is he.

Fesser: Ah, but the identity of both of you is certainly in question.

Socrates: To you, perhaps, not to me.

Fesser: What did you mean when you said you met him?

Socrates: That I met something more than a pretense, just as you are now meeting something more than a pretense of Socrates.

Fesser: Just as . . . oh, I see. Yes. Very clever, Socrates.

Socrates: You are mistaken on both counts.

Fesser: What do you mean?

Socrates: You do not see, and I am not very clever.

Fesser: You mean you're claiming real presence for both Jesus and Socrates?

Socrates: You could put it that way, yes.

Fesser: Do you claim to have had a mystical experience?

Socrates: I claim to have met a person. Is that a mystical experience? I suppose you might say so, in a sense.

Fesser: For the first time you are not wholly making sense to me, Socrates.

Ahmen: Well, he's making sense to me, more than he ever did before. He even *looks* different today. And yet—how to say it?— Socrates, you look more yourself than ever, more Socratic, somehow.

Socrates [firmly]: We are not here to look at me but to look at him. Here in this course and here in this world.

Fesser: Then let's do just that. Socrates, tell us, did you react differently to Jesus than the Jews did? And if so, do you think that was due to your cultural difference, your Greek background?

Socrates: That is still a question about *me*, not about him. But to answer it, I believe one of the sayings in this book goes something like this: "In relation to Christ there is no difference between Jew and Greek." Isn't that right?

Fesser: Yes, that's in St. Paul. Could you tell us what you think it means?

Socrates: That Jesus elicits the same basic reactions from anyone, I think. For instance, I quite understood the reaction of the Jews to him, though I am a Greek.

Fesser: Which Jews? Which reaction?

Socrates: A good question. There were different groups and different reactions. And I think I understand them all. First, the scholars, the scribes, the Jewish philosophers. They were simply astonished. "Never spoke any man like this man"—that was their reaction. I understand why. Here was something more than a philosopher who was nevertheless the world's greatest philosopher. He cut through their questions as the sun cuts through layers of fog.

Fesser: And the other groups?

Socrates: Two of them were the Sanhedrin and the Herodians, who, I take it, were the political party in power, in cahoots with Herod the king. In other words, the religious and political establishments. Both felt profoundly threatened by this man. In Athens they even felt threatened by me, so I can certainly understand how they would feel threatened by him.

Bertha: Why did they feel so threatened? I never understood that.

Socrates: Then you never understood him. The establishment is canny, like an animal with instincts to identify its natural enemy, or like a body rejecting foreign tissue. They were like water and he was like fire; if they do not put him out, he puts them out. He often spoke of his radical newness, for instance, when he said that old skins cannot contain new wine.

Fesser: And was there a fourth group?

Socrates: Yes, the people, the masses, who worshiped him one week and screamed for his crucifixion the next. The fickle mob— it all sounded very familiar to me, as if Jerusalem were a democracy just like Athens.

Bertha: Are you saying democracy is evil?

Fesser: Excuse me, Bertha, but let's not get distracted by that question, all right? Socrates, did you see any other reactions from any other group?

Socrates: Perhaps a fifth group were the religious Jews who were clear-minded enough to realize that they had to either worship him, if he was the God he claimed to be, or crucify him, if he wasn't. For Moses commanded the death penalty for blasphemy, and if he wasn't God, then he was the greatest of blasphemers. But these Jews weren't sure which of the two he was. So they listened to him, watched him and waited, questioningly.

Fesser: And I suppose you fit into this group, Socrates? The questioners, the seekers, the agnostics?

Socrates: At first, yes. Like Nicodemus.

Ahmen: Why not the sixth group, Socrates, his disciples?

Socrates: I thought at first that that would be the least likely group to identify with because of the immense improbability of their central belief, that this man Jesus was literally God in the flesh.

Ahmen: Why did that seem so improbable?

Socrates: Don't you see? It's like saying a square is at the same time a circle. How can the divine nature coexist with the human nature? How can the same man be both eternal and temporal, immortal and mortal, divine and human? It certainly seems to be a very large and very obvious contradiction, to anyone who knows a little logic.

Thomas: Right on, Socrates!

Socrates: No, Thomas, right off. Off the main point. For what I met when I read this book was not an essence, or a concept, or a nature, but a person.

Thomas [shocked]: So you just gave up your reason?

Socrates [sternly]: Certainly not! But does it not seem that reason itself must recognize something beyond it?

Thomas: No. Why?

Socrates: For one thing, something has to *have* reason, does it not?

Thomas: What do you mean? What something?

Socrates: We reason because we are persons, isn't that so? Things of a rational nature?

Thomas: Yes.

Socrates: But the haver is not the had, is it?

Thomas: I'm not sure what that means.

Socrates: The subject is not the object.

Thomas: I'm still not sure I get your point.

Socrates: It is not reason that has reason; it is we.

Thomas: Oh. Of course. So what?

Socrates: So however perfectly and however high you build the temple of reason, it has to have something underneath it, something like the earth. And it has to have a builder, a person.

Thomas: Socrates, this just doesn't sound like you.

Socrates: I am not abandoning any of my former philosophy, I think, only becoming clearer about an addition to it. All I am saying is that a person is more than just a nature, an essence. A person *has* a nature or essence.

Thomas: O.K. I accept the distinction. So what?

Socrates: What I met in this book was not a definition of an essence, but a person—a person who obviously had the human essence and claimed also to have the divine essence.

Thomas: O.K., so you met a person. But his claim is ridiculous.

Socrates: It is certainly very shocking and *seems*, on the face of it, ridiculous. But you know my attitude toward seeming.

Thomas: But how can one person have two natures? It's not possible.

Socrates: That possibility or impossibility has to be examined, surely. But something else has to be examined too, and that is what I did—something actual, not just possible. I mean the person Jesus.

So I thought I should look at this one person first, and then look at the two essences a bit more—although I already looked last week at the divine essence according to your Old Testament, and I have been looking at the human essence all my life. The first and greatest commandment for me was "Know thyself."

Fesser: Socrates, I think that with this "person" and "nature" talk, your knowledge of the history of Christian theology and the creeds is tempting you to commit anachronisms. Do you really think the real Socrates would have come up with the Nicean-Chalcedonian solution to the Christological conundrum?

Socrates: I'm sorry, but I haven't the foggiest idea what you're talking about. All I know is that I met a person.

Thomas: I think you gave up your reason.

Socrates: Do you have to give up your reason to meet a person?

Thomas: What did you do with your reason, then?

Socrates: I was led by the river of reason to the ocean of the whole person, to something that is more than reason but not less.

Thomas: And once you were swept into the ocean, your feet left the ground and you were carried by the waves?

Socrates: The metaphor seems apt.

Thomas: Then you did give up your reason, your feet.

Socrates: Indeed not. Do swimmers lose their feet? On the contrary, they use their feet while swimming too.

Thomas: You mean you're still reasoning even after you took the leap of faith?

Socrates: Something like that. And even a leap has to begin with your feet. And when you end a leap and come down, you have to come down on your feet again.

Thomas: Does that analogy mean that you think there were rational motives for your belief and rational explanations for it afterwards?

Socrates: Yes, that is what it means.

Thomas: This I've gotta see!

Socrates: Yes, you do.

Fesser: Socrates, you described your experience as being swept into the sea. I don't understand—do you mean that you had a mystical experience? Or was it just a matter of sitting down and thinking rationally?

Socrates: I do not see why you call meeting a person a mystical experience. Are you having one now?

Fesser: But I'm meeting a real person. You only read a book.

Socrates: No. I did not only read a book. I met a real person. The book was not the object of my experience, only the medium, or the occasion.

Ahmen: Or the sacrament, perhaps?

Socrates: What is that, please?

Ahmen: The official definition is "sign that effects what it signifies."

Socrates: That is well put. The words were signs that signified, but they also somehow helped to make present the person they signified, like a catalyst in a chemical reaction.

Fesser: And you believe what this person says?

Socrates: Yes, I believe he is the one he said he is. I will tell you why in a minute.

Bertha: So, Socrates, you have become a Christian. How interesting!

Socrates: Interesting? How can you speak of it as if I had only changed my philosophy?

Bertha: Isn't that what you did?

Socrates: Is being born a change of philosophy? If so, I suppose you could say I only changed my philosophy.

Bertha: Being born?

Socrates: It is the most accurate of all images. That is why he used it, I think, when he spoke to the Jewish philosopher and seeker Nicodemus. It is an accurate image because only birth is as radical a change as this—a change not only in one's thought but in one's being, and a change not just from less being to more being, but from nonbeing to being. Something new was born in me. He himself was born in me, as the book says.

Bertha: I don't understand. *[Furrowed brow, interest.]*

Socrates: I see. Do any of you understand? *[Pleadingly]* Professor?

Fesser: There are many ways of understanding any image, Socrates. Surely you know that.

Socrates: Of course I do. I was not speaking of understanding the symbol but of understanding the thing it symbolizes.

Fesser: The thing it symbolizes?

Socrates: What do you mean?

Fesser: Do you assume there must be only one level, one dimension, of reality?

Socrates: I never dreamed I would pass up the opportunity to angle for such a metaphysical fish as that question. But that is just what I am about to do. For I have met a whale, and even the fishing apparatus of metaphysics is inadequate to catch this whale. I think we have pursued our question with an admirably single-minded intent so far, many times refusing long and attractive detours into important and fascinating side roads. Even this question is such a side road, I think. I mean the question of what *reality* means, and whether or not we can speak of such a thing as *the* reality. Rather, I must ask another question. I fear it will be misunderstood and prove embarrassing, so please be patient with me and try very hard not to misunderstand my motives in asking it.

Class: Sure, Socrates. *[Accommodating, open, inviting looks.]*

Bertha [impatient, interested]: What's the question?

Socrates: Where are the Christians? *[Whole class looks shocked and puzzled.]*

Bertha: What do you mean? They're all over the place.

Socrates: This place?

Bertha: Of course this place, and many other places too.

Socrates: Then there is something I do not understand.

Bertha: What's that?

Socrates: If you are all Christians, if some of you are Christians, if any of you are Christians—how could your life be the same? How could you look the same, talk the same, think the same? How could the born child so closely resemble the unborn child? How could your life be so . . . so bland, if this incredible thing is true?

Molly: Socrates, are you putting us down?

Socrates: Alas, that is what I feared you would think. That's why the question is so embarrassing. Look here, I am certainly no expert in this Christianity thing; I have only discovered it in the last few days, so far be it from me to tell you or anyone what it all really amounts to. But this book of yours does tell us—all of us, me as well as you—what it all amounts to. And if everything in this book is true, then what it amounts to compared to everything else I have ever known is like a whale compared to minnows.

Fesser: It's nice of you to take the New Testament so seriously, Socrates, but . . .

Socrates: Nice? Did you say nice?

Molly: Oh, Socrates, don't be so negative. We're all happy for you if you've found happiness.

Socrates: Even happiness is hardly ever spoken of in this book, but rather joy. Do any of you understand that distinction? *[All look blank.]* Did you all read the New Testament?

All: Of course.

Socrates: Perhaps you "of coursed" it. Is that what it means to "take a course" here?

Fesser [annoyed yet interested]: Exactly what do you find missing, Socrates?

Socrates: Everything!

Fesser: Surely you of all people could explain a bit more clearly.

Socrates: I shall certainly try. See here, if I understand this book, it claims that the supreme Creator-God became a man so that men and women could become gods and goddesses. "Partakers in the divine nature," it says. How could anything be the same after that, if it really happens?

Fesser: Oh, well, now, that is something of a bone of contention. Should we interpret the metaphor of participating in the divine nature to refer to a literal, historical event, or is it instead a mythological expression, not to be taken literally?

Socrates: A myth? Do you think it is a myth?

Fesser: Some do, some don't.

Socrates: And you? What do you think?

Fesser [uncomfortable]: That is not the issue here. This is an academic classroom, not a revival meeting. *[Some giggle.]*

Bertha [trying to bail Fesser out]: Socrates, are you asking why we aren't all saints?

Socrates: No, not if you mean heroes of perfection. The people in your Bible were not that. All of them had flaws—unlike the heroes and heroines of the fiction of my culture. That is one of the reasons your book seems to be factual, by the way. No, I'm asking about something else, something that's hard to define but easy to recognize, I think, though the only place I have recognized it so far is in this book.

Let me put it this way. When I read about this man Jesus and about his disciples and about his "called-out-ones" (that's what *church* means, doesn't it?)—when I read this, I find something so unmistakable, so distinctive, so strong and full of life and joy, that it's like the noonday sun. If all these things really happened, then it's no wonder that the whole world was turned upside down, as your book says, even the hard-nosed Roman world. It's no wonder the people who met Christ either worshiped him or crucified him. And it's no wonder the people who met his disciples either believed them and worshiped him, or didn't believe them and persecuted them for telling this abominable, insane lie. It's got to be all or nothing, either-or.

Fesser: Are you defending fanaticism, Socrates?

Socrates: No.

Fesser: What, then?

Socrates: Something more like marriage. In-loveness. Fidelity.

Fesser: And what do you think you see around you instead?

Socrates: Scholarship. Teachers and students playing at a game, like children playing safari while there is a real lion lurking in their own front yard. You think you are studying a dead man, don't you?—a man like myself as I was until a few days ago, rather than someone alive, and present, and active, as I am now. Isn't that how you see it?

Bertha: But Socrates, Jesus isn't here as you are here.

Socrates: Your book says that he is. His disciples believed and acted as if he was. He himself promised to be. If it's not a myth, if he really rose from the dead, then he's not dead, but alive, like an animal—at least as alive as an animal. But you seem to be studying him as if he were a picture or a bump on a log. Have you ever sat down on a bump on a log and found it to be a frog? Or perhaps the whole log turned out to be an alligator? "Look out! It's alive!" you say. I have not heard anyone say anything like that here.

Bertha: And that's what happened to you? The alligator came alive?

Socrates: Yes. And . . . not to you?

Bertha [evasive but interested]: Well, in a sense . . .

Socrates: Do you or do you not believe that he really rose from the dead?

Bertha: In a sense . . .

Socrates: What sense?

Bertha: Everything rises from the dead. He's the archetype? Surely you of all people understand archetypes, Platonic Ideas.

Socrates: I do indeed—so well, in fact, that I think I can recognize what is an archetype and what is an individual entity or event. I think I can distinguish Life from an animal, or Justice from a ruler, or War from a particular war. And the clear claim of your Scriptures is that the birth and life and death and resurrection and ascension of this person Jesus who claimed to be God, all happened, once, in history. But an archetype does not *happen;* it simply *is.* It is an eternal truth, a universal meaning, a perpetual possibility.

Fesser: I think we should all be sure we're clear about that difference, Socrates, because it seems to be a fundamental difference between the mindset of the Jews and that of the Greeks.

Socrates: I don't know about that, about mindsets. My problem now is first of all simply to understand him.

Fesser: But you did use the distinction between archetype and event to do that.

Socrates: Only because Bertha did. She interpreted Jesus as an archetype.

Fesser: Well, since the distinction is on the floor, could you give us a clearer account of it?

Socrates: Easily. Let us say that the rules of trigonometry are archetypal, while the Great Pyramid is historical. Or the sun is historical, while Apollo is an archetype, a mythic symbol for spiritual enlightenment, which is symbolized by physical sight, or sunlight.

Fesser: And you are denying that Jesus is an archetype?

Socrates: No, I am saying that he is historical. Perhaps he is an archetype too.

Fesser: How could anything be both? You just set up a clear distinction between the two.

Socrates: Is that not the whole point of the Incarnation? That eternity became time, God became man, myth became historical?

Fesser: So he *is* an archetype.

Socrates: Apparently so. But clearly he is historical too, or the texts simply lie.

Bertha: But Socrates, don't you see?—the really important thing is the archetypal. Jesus stands for Life. Life is the really important thing. That's why we celebrate Easter in the spring, when the earth wakes up with new life. That's why we have Easter eggs and Easter bunnies—symbols of new life.

Socrates: If I understand this book correctly, you have it exactly backwards.

Bertha: Backwards? How do you mean?

Socrates: From its perspective, spring must be said to come at Easter time, not Easter at spring time.

Bertha: I don't understand, Socrates.

Socrates: The new life on earth symbolizes the new life from heaven. But you seem to have turned the symbolism upside down, making heaven symbolize earth, as if Jesus were just another Easter bunny.

Fesser: But surely, Socrates, you see the profound symbolic value of the resurrection? Surely you don't want to reduce it to brute fact? Surely the insistence on literal historicity is missing the point?

Socrates: What point? What is the point I am missing?

Fesser: Life itself.

Socrates: The archetype?

Fesser: Yes.

Socrates: But I affirm that. I say the archetype itself somehow became historical, incarnated itself. My problem is not, it seems to me, that I am missing something, that I see only half the picture, but that I have too much, too many halves. I do not understand how the two can be one, how a man can be both God and man. But clearly that is what this book says. I think you have read some other book instead.

Fesser [stiffly]: I've spent my career on this book. But there are many different ways to interpret it. You're just being hermeneutically unsophisticated.

Socrates: May I ask you an unsophisticated question?

Fesser: Certainly.

Socrates: Do you believe Jesus really rose from the tomb or not?

Fesser: Socrates, I really think you're missing the point.

Socrates: Professor, you're not answering my question.

Fesser: It's not as simple as you make it.

Socrates: I don't see why not. Either he rose from the tomb or he didn't.

Fesser: Ah, but you're neglecting the whole dimension of meaning and interpretation. What does resurrection *mean?*

Socrates: Clearly, whatever else it may mean, it means that a man who was dead came back to life again. What do you think it means? Bunnies?

Fesser: Socrates, there was a philosopher named Bultmann who said that even if the bones of the dead Jesus were found tomorrow in a tomb in Palestine, all the essentials of Christianity would still remain unchanged. I think you are ignoring those essentials.

Socrates: That may be what Bultmann said, but it is clearly not what this book of yours says. "If Christ is not risen, your faith is vain." That doesn't sound like "all the essentials unchanged" to me.

Fesser: Socrates, I'd just like to run something by you to see what you make of it. It's an interpretation of the resurrection, O.K.? Let's compare it with Plato's philosophy. Plato's magnum opus, the *Republic*, centers on the thesis that philosophers must become kings or kings become philosophers, and thus political power and philosophical wisdom and goodness become one. That's his central prescription for utopia, or at least for a good, just, healthy society. All right?

Socrates: What does that have to do with Jesus' resurrection?

Fesser: The resurrection makes the same point in a different way. The point is the union of power and goodness. Jesus is the perfectly good man, the ideal man, the wise and moral man. The resurrection is power, the power of goodness, the union of power with goodness. Death represents weakness and defeat; life represents power and victory. The problem of human life—the central problem of human life, really—is that goodness seems weak and gets defeated. Good guys are kicked around by bad guys. The resurrection reverses that. It symbolizes the strength, the power of moral goodness over evil, by the power of Jesus' life over death. The resurrection is the unification of the two great forces in the universe, power and goodness.

Molly: Ooh, I like that—unification.

Socrates [ignoring Molly]: But Professor, if it didn't really happen, then goodness isn't really unified with power, is it?

Fesser: It doesn't have to happen for the meaning to be intact. An archetype doesn't have to be incarnated to be an archetype. The meaning is the thing, the really important thing, not the historical literalism.

Socrates: Shall we examine this interpretation?

Fesser: Please.

Socrates: The meaning of the resurrection, you say, is the union of goodness with power?

Fesser: Yes.

Socrates: Not just goodness, but goodness united with power?

Fesser: Yes. And not just power, but power united with goodness. The power of goodness.

Socrates: And you say that the resurrection did not really happen?

Fesser: No, I did not say that. I said it is not necessary to interpret it literally.

Socrates: To interpret it literally—this is to believe that it really happened, in history, on the earth, physically, biologically, in Jesus' body and not just in other people's minds, is that correct?

Fesser: Yes.

Socrates: And you say that the meaning of the resurrection remains even if the historical happening is no longer believed?

Fesser: The literal, biological, historical happening, yes.

Socrates: Ah, but if it didn't happen in history, then it is only a myth, an archetype.

Fesser: Yes.

Socrates: A beautiful fairy tale.

Fesser: You might call it that.

Socrates: Jesus the historical person did not have the power to rise from the dead, but Jesus the myth does.

Fesser: Yes.

Socrates: And rising from the dead means power?

Fesser: Yes.

Socrates: And Jesus represents goodness?

Fesser: Yes.

Socrates: Then if Jesus didn't really conquer death, it follows that goodness does not really have power. In that case, the meaning is not intact, is it? For if the resurrection really happened, the meaning is that goodness has power, and if it didn't really happen, then goodness does not have power. Does not that follow?

Fesser: No, Socrates. It needn't be historically true, only mythically true—a fairy tale, as you put it. You don't expect of a fairy tale that it be historically accurate.

Socrates: Ah, but *this* fairy tale, even as a tale, is different from all other fairy tales, according to your interpretation; for it is not only about goodness but about the union of goodness with power. The meaning of other fairy tales is unchanged whether the tales have the power of history or not, but the meaning of this fairy tale *is* the union of archetype with history, myth with fact, goodness with power. So how can its meaning survive the loss of half of its meaning, namely its history, its power?

Fesser: Hmmm. There does seem to be a self-referential inconsistency in my hermeneutic.

Socrates: I suppose that is as close as a professor gets to "repent and believe"?

Fesser [polite laughter]: What do *you* think, Socrates? What do you say? Why do you think the resurrection has to be literal?

Socrates: I? About this thing I only know what your Scriptures say. My answer to your question is nothing original and quite obvious.

Fesser: Frankly, it's not obvious to me.

Socrates: Then you must not have read the book.

Fesser: Don't be arrogant, Socrates. In fact I have read the book at least a hundred times, and I have written a dozen books and nearly a hundred articles about it.

Socrates: Then you surely must know the answer it gives to your question.

Fesser: I would still like to hear your answer, Socrates.

Socrates: All right, but my answer is not mine, but Scripture's. Yours, on the other hand, seems to be not Scripture's, but yours. And since we have all read the book and know its answer, should we not hear your addition to it rather than my repetition of it?

Fesser [deliberately, forcing a smile]: I would like to hear your answer, Socrates.

Socrates: Very well. The question is why the resurrection must be literal, correct?

Fesser: Correct.

Socrates: First, because it proves Jesus' claim to divinity: only a God can conquer death. Second, because it is the completion of his task, his purpose, the reason he became a man—to save man from death and the origin of death, sin. That is what the New Testament says. I do not claim to understand all that this means, for instance just how it works, how the work of Jesus' living and dying and rising saves us from sin and death. But surely what I said is simply what it says.

Fesser: There are other interpretations, which emphasize other dimensions of Jesus . . .

Socrates: Instead of this one?

Fesser: Yes.

Socrates: I don't understand. What I just said is on nearly every page of the New Testament. Even a child can see that.

Ahmen: Perhaps only a child.

Fesser [with withering glance at Ahmen]: Socrates, frankly I'm surprised at you. I had thought that with all the wealth of mythic culture you brought to us you would be much more nuanced, more sophisticated, more literary in approaching this whole thing of the resurrection. You seem to have become a fundamentalist.

Socrates: There goes that terrible term again! Does it mean neglecting the symbolic dimension?

Fesser: Yes, among other things.

Socrates: Then I do not want to be a fundamentalist. For I certainly don't want to do that.

Fesser: What do you think of your Greek myths, Socrates?

Socrates: They seem to me to be very much like the Jewish prophets I read last week in the Old Testament in one way. They point forward to Jesus.

Fesser: How's that?

Socrates: Many of them were about a dying and rising god. Some even said that by that death and resurrection the god somehow won life for the world.

Fesser [brightening]: Oh, well then, the Christ event isn't so unique after all. It is a universal, mythic archetype.

Socrates: Indeed it is. But it is also unique, it seems.

Fesser: Please tell us how.

Socrates: It is so simple that I shall need a long time to say it.

Fesser: Go ahead.

Socrates: It is true. It happened. It may be myth, but it is myth become fact. It may be an archetype, but it incarnated itself in history. You see, I had already known the basic outline of the myth. In a sense I learned nothing new from your New Testament. In another sense, everything was new. It was in a new place, the earth rather than the heavens of eternal, archetypal truth. It was as if a story that I had always heard in vague whispers suddenly took the utterly clear and solid form of *happening.* Myths do not *happen;* they simply are. Try to imagine what you would feel if you actually met in your world one of your fairy tales come true, exactly—no, much *more* exactly than in the tale. That is what I found when I read this book.

Fesser: So you now see one of your myths as prophetic of Christ?

Socrates: All the myths seem to point to him in one way or another. I think I understood my own myths for the first time when I read the New Testament, rather as one would understand the meaning of a confused dream for the first time if he woke to find the very things he had dreamed about there in the real world.

Fesser: How had you previously understood your myths, Socrates?

Socrates: Wrongly. My rational mind dismissed them as mere fables. I thought I could squeeze the moral truths out of them as you squeeze juice out of a fruit, and express those truths as philosophy, leaving behind the dry rind of myth. Yet even as I did this, something in me warned against it, as if there was something that I was missing, something even more precious in the rind than in the juice. Now I see what it was—not an *it* but a *he.*

Fesser: You seem to be saying that you find prophets outside Israel—in your pagan tradition too. Is that correct?

Socrates: Yes.

Fesser: Then you believe that all religions are valid ways to God?

Socrates: I don't know what you mean by "valid."

Fesser: True to a certain extent.

Socrates: I would not put it that way. Jesus did not say, "The truth to a certain extent will make you free to a certain extent."

Fesser: But all religions have something of value in them, at any rate, don't you think?

Socrates: I do not know all religions, only a few.

Fesser: And the few you do know? What of them?

Socrates: It seems to me that they all contain some truth, if that's what you're asking.

Fesser: Yes, that's what I'm asking.

Socrates: But that sounds rather trivial. It is quite difficult to say very much without saying some truth, after all.

Fesser: Don't you think the myths contain some very profound truths?

Socrates: Yes, though often mixed with very silly errors and expressed obscurely.

Fesser: So the myths were prophets outside Israel.

Socrates: Surely. Don't your Scriptures say as much? "God has not left himself without witness," or something like that.

Fesser: And what about the philosophers? Do you think they were prophetic too?

Socrates: A philosopher is a lover of wisdom, by definition. And all wisdom resides in the mind of God, does it not? So in seeking wisdom, a philosopher is seeking God, whether he knows it or not.

Fesser: And do you think any of the philosophers found the God they sought?

Socrates: I think they found some important truths about him.

Fesser: So you would see the Hebrew prophets, the Greek philosophers, and the worldwide myth-makers as all pointing to God.

Socrates: Yes.

Fesser: They are all quite similar, then.

Molly: I knew it. Socrates discovers the principle, the unity!

Socrates: They seem to have their divine goal in common. But they also seem to have important differences. In clarity, for one thing—the prophets seem the clearest, the philosophers next, and the myth-makers last. In adequacy, for another thing—here again, the prophets seem to tell us the most about God. And perhaps here the philosophers tell us the least. I had always thought that we philosophers knew more of God than the myth-makers did, but now I am not so sure. Perhaps our maxims were clear but thin, like thin soup, while the myths were dark but thick, like stew, or blood.

Fesser: Could you say these three traditions were like three rivers all running into the same sea?

Socrates: Yes, from three different directions, which would be the three parts of the soul. The river of philosophy would spring from the mountains of the soul, the intellect. The river of the prophets, the moralists, would spring from the middle part of the soul, the heart, or will. This is like the slopes. And the myths spring from the marshes and steamy lowlands of the soul, which are alive with every form of life, good and bad.

Fesser: But any one of the three rivers, then, can carry you to its common destination, the divine sea?

Socrates: I do not know that. Perhaps the river of philosophy is too cold, too rocky, or too shallow for most people to sail it successfully. Perhaps the river of myth is too muddy, too swampy, for most of its travelers to get unstuck and reach the sea. Perhaps only the river of the prophets is pure and clear and deep and straight and safe for travel.

Fesser: Are you saying you can't get to God by these other routes?

Socrates: I do not know that either. I have only recently come to know your Scriptures. How could I solve the problem of compar-ative religions, as you call it, when I am only a beginner in one of the things compared?

Fesser: All right, let's not get distracted into that problem either. Socrates, when I asked you why you thought the resurrection had to be literal, you answered that it proved Jesus' divinity, isn't that right?

Socrates: Yes.

Fesser: Do I understand you correctly—you're interpreting both resurrection and divinity literally, aren't you?

Socrates: Yes.

Fesser: Are you aware that there are many good Christian thinkers who don't? And with good reason, I think. One of their reasons that should appeal to you, Socrates, is this: that the soul is more important than the body, and therefore it's sort of low and crass and crude and even vulgar to insist on the physical aspects of the resurrection, as if the meaning of the resurrection were the biological reunification of the molecules in Jesus' body. Don't you think that view deserves a hearing?

Socrates: All views deserve a hearing—one, at least. Whether they deserve a second can be determined by the first. Shall we investigate?

Fesser: Investigate away, Socrates.

Socrates: Well, then, if Jesus did not literally rise from the dead, what did?

Fesser: I don't understand. Why must there be some *what* that rose from the dead literally?

Socrates: Why use the term *resurrection* if nothing happened?

Fesser: Oh, something happened, all right. The real resurrection happened in the hearts and minds and lives of Jesus' disciples. They changed from fearful, confused people to confident, purposeful people who spiritually conquered the world.

Socrates: What changed them?

Fesser: The resurrection of Easter faith.

Socrates: But if Easter did not really happen, their Easter faith was a delusion. Did a delusion conquer the world?

Fesser: No, Easter faith is Jesus' message and way of life, not a delusion. *That* lives forever, even if his body is dead.

Socrates: And Jesus' message is to have faith, to live by faith?

Fesser: Yes. Now you see it.

Socrates: I see, but there is no *it* to see. It is like a hall of mirrors. What you speak of is faith in faith. That's like being in love with love instead of with a real person, is it not? Surely not the same thing. If there is no resurrection, where is the object of Easter faith? And without an object, how can there be faith?

Fesser: Perhaps there is a logical difficulty there. I think my colleague in the philosophy department could handle that one by his theory of levels of language. It's a matter of first-order questions versus second-order questions.

Socrates: It certainly seems to be a matter of whether a dead body came to life again. How remarkably easily it becomes only a question of language!

Fesser: It's a question of belief and interpretation.

Socrates: But surely there are three kinds of questions?—I mean, first, questions about what happens or happened in the real world; and second, questions about what happens in people's minds, what they think or believe about the world; and third, questions of language, communicating those beliefs and thoughts. Must we not face all three questions?

Fesser: Fine. But you seem to be concentrating only on the first question and ignoring the others, especially the second, what goes on in someone's mind and heart and life. There's where the real drama happens, the thing that concerns us most.

Socrates: I do not wish to ignore that question, only to relate it to the first. Is that a legitimate thing to do, to relate these two questions? Do we not want to do just that, to relate what we believe to the real world?

Fesser: Of course.

Socrates: Then let us do just that. Let us relate the two questions of what happened in the real world and what was believed. All right?

Fesser: All right.

Socrates: Each question has two possible answers, yes or no. There are two possibilities in the real world: either Jesus really rose or he did not. And there are two possibilities in the disciples' minds: either they believed that Jesus rose or they did not. Thus there are four possible combinations. *First*, that he rose and they believed that he rose. This is what your Scriptures say. *Second*, that he rose but they did not believe it. In this case, they lied when they wrote the Gospels, for they said that they believed even though they did not. *Third*, that Jesus did not rise and they didn't believe that he did. In that case again they lied, both about the facts and about their belief. *Fourth*, that Jesus didn't rise but the disciples thought he did—which is what you say I think. In that case again they did not tell the truth, although it was not a deliberate lie but simply superstition and ignorance.

Fesser: What's the point of this analysis, Socrates?

Socrates: That in three of these four cases, it is a falsehood that transformed lives and conquered the world—in two of the three cases a deliberate falsehood. I do not see how a falsehood can have such noble consequences.

Fesser: Myths are often very successful, Socrates.

Socrates: I was not thinking of success, but of joy and wisdom and moral power. How can a lie make a sinner into a saint?

Fesser: And how can anyone be sure what really happened two thousand years ago in a tomb?

Socrates: You answer a question with another question. That is a clever way of evading the question. But if I try to answer yours, will you try to answer mine?

Fesser [uncomfortably]: Yes, of course.

Socrates: Well, then, we may not know what happened inside the tomb, but we know what happened outside the tomb. This faith in Jesus and the resurrection conquered the world. It seems nearly certain that whether Jesus rose or not, his disciples really believed that he did. What else gave them fearlessness in the face of persecution and suffering and death? If they knew the resurrection was a lie, what would give them the courage to die for a lie? If they were not assured by Jesus' rising that death was no longer to be feared, what made them so fearless in the face of death?

Fesser: It was the example of Jesus, Jesus' radical new way of life.

Socrates: His ethical teachings?

Fesser: Yes.

Socrates: I do not see how they are so radically new. I had already found most of them in the Jewish prophets, and many of them in my own mind and my own philosophy.

Fesser: It's true that anticipations of many of Jesus' ethical teachings can be found in the prophets and pagan traditions. But Jesus lived these teachings to the fullest. "He went about doing good," to put it simply.

Socrates: What good did he do? Miracles, healings, raising the dead. The Gospels tell us little else that he did.

Fesser: I'll admit that the record—if we are to believe it—does portray a literal resurrection and disciples who believe a literal resurrection. But you can't prove it really happened just from that. The disciples were peasants, not philosophers, after all. There's no need for us to be so crassly concerned with the literal and the material, as they apparently were, don't you think—you, of all people, Socrates? You who so strongly affirmed the superiority of the soul over the body?

Socrates: Perhaps I am learning something I did not know before. But to answer your question, yes, I do think that there is at least one very good reason for being so crassly concerned with the material.

Fesser [surprised]: What is that?

Socrates: Is death a crass and crude and material problem?

Fesser: I'm not quite sure what you mean . . .

Socrates: Does a corpse stink?

Fesser [slight smile]: I think I see what you mean . . . But I expected you as a philosopher to seek for a more philosophical understanding of the resurrection than that.

Socrates: A philosopher must be logical, must he not?

Fesser: Yes.

Socrates: And to be logical is to be consistent?

Fesser: Yes.

Socrates: And to be consistent is to seek for a solution that is appropriate to the problem?

Fesser: Yes.

Socrates: And death is a problem to man?

Fesser: Certainly.

Socrates: And death is a literal, material fact, is it not? Something you might call crass and crude and vulgar?

Fesser: Yes.

Socrates: Then the solution to this problem, if it is to be philosophical, must be a crass and crude and vulgar and material solution—like a real resurrection.

Fesser: Oh, that's a clever a priori argument, Socrates. But we have to look at data, facts, the real world.

Socrates: Exactly what I thought I was doing.

Fesser: But scientifically speaking, don't you think a nonmiraculous explanation seems at least much more likely than a miraculous resurrection?

Socrates: No, I do not.

Fesser: Why not?

Socrates: If there was no resurrection of Jesus' body, there seem to be three questions that are extremely difficult to answer without absurdity. First, who moved the stone? Second, who got the body? Third, why did the disciples invent this lie?

Fesser: To take your first question first, the disciples could have moved the stone, couldn't they? Isn't that much more likely than an angel doing it? If you saw a huge stone in your back yard moved overnight, would you think an angel had done it?

Socrates: No. But my back yard is not guarded by Roman soldiers.

Fesser: The soldiers could have been bribed or drugged.

Socrates: If the disciples had the stone moved, what did they do with his body?

Fesser: Hid it, I suppose. Buried it.

Socrates: So they concocted the whole thing as a lie.

Fesser: On this hypothesis, yes. Mind you, I'm not dogmatizing about it. I just think we should consider every hypothesis and not let traditional pieties prevent us from keeping an open mind on the subject—on every subject. Don't you agree with that approach?

Socrates: I do. Everything should be considered. But some things should be rejected after being considered, don't you think?

Fesser: I've never been comfortable with negative attitudes and heresy-hunting.

Socrates: Do you mean no idea should ever be denied? Then how can any be affirmed? If X is not false, how can non-X be true?

Fesser: Oh, I'm not disputing the laws of logic . . .

Socrates: I should hope not!

Fesser: I'm just insisting on an open mind at all times. And what about you?

Socrates: I do not think we should have an open mind at all times.

Fesser [shocked]: Socrates! How could you?

Socrates: To ring a change on the metaphor Ahmen quoted from Mr. Chesterton, isn't an open mind rather like an open door? It should be open to all visitors. But once they come, you must decide which of them should stay and which should not. Do you want robbers and rapists to remain in your house? Do you want lies to remain in your mind?

Fesser: Oh, I see. I think you think *I* think the resurrection was a *lie*. Is that it?

Socrates: Let me sort out all those *thinks* . . . I don't know what I think about what you think. But what do *you* think about the *resurrection*? Did it really happen?

Fesser: Yes! But not in the material world. In the spiritual world, in the hearts and in the lives of the disciples.

Socrates: If I say something really happened in the world when it didn't, am I not telling a lie?

Fesser: No, you may be telling a myth.

Socrates: And the people who believed this myth—did they think it was a truth or a myth?

Fesser: Most of them believed it to be literally true.

Socrates: So most of the millions of Christians throughout history believed that Jesus literally rose from the dead?

Fesser: Yes.

Socrates: But Jesus' original disciples knew better? They must have, if they moved the stone and stole the body.

Fesser: Perhaps.

Socrates: Then here is the question that seems unanswerable: What did these disciples get out of their lie? When someone deceives another, the deceiver is always motivated by some thought of advantage. What advantage did the disciples gain by their conspiracy?

Ahmen: I will answer that question for you, Socrates. I'll tell you what they got out of it. They got mocked, hated, sneered at, jeered at, exiled, deprived of their property, their reputation and their civil rights; they got imprisoned, whipped, tortured, clubbed to a pulp, stoned, beheaded, sawed in pieces, boiled in oil, crucified, fed to lions and cut to ribbons by gladiators. That's what they got out of it.

Socrates: Is this true, Professor?

Fesser: Many of the early Christians were martyrs, yes.

Socrates: And under torture none ever confessed that it was all a lie, a myth, a fabrication?

Fesser: No.

Socrates: This is amazing! The human heart is exceedingly fickle, is it not? Especially the heart of a liar? I do not understand what could have made them endure such torture except their certainty that Jesus really did rise and that they would too. If they didn't believe in the resurrection, why would they give up the only life they knew was real for nothing?

Fesser: That's a good question, but it doesn't prove that the resurrection literally happened.

Socrates: It seems to prove this, at least—that if the miracle of the resurrection didn't really happen, then an even more incredible miracle happened.

Fesser: What do you mean?

Socrates: Twelve Jewish peasants invented the world's most fantastic and successful lie for no reason at all and died for it willingly and joyfully, as martyrs. As did millions of others.

Fesser: That's sort of what I've been trying to tell you, Socrates. The real miracle is in lives, not in molecules.

Socrates: But what motivated the miracle in lives? An effect must have a cause at least as great as itself, isn't that true? I do not see what could have caused this miracle of changed lives except an even greater miracle. The resurrection would have such power, but how could a lie have such power?

Fesser: Not a lie, a myth.

Socrates: Myth indeed! It seems much more likely to me, Professor, that your idea is the myth, and that the miracle is the sober fact.

Fesser [riled]: Thomas, what do you think about Socrates' arguments? Has he convinced you? And if not, why not?

Thomas [surprised to be picked on to bail out Fesser]: Me? Uh . . . well, to be honest, Professor, his arguments make more sense than I had thought. I have to do much more thinking on this subject.

Fesser: I'm surprised to hear that from you, Thomas.

Thomas: Why? Haven't I always been open-minded?

Fesser: Oh, that's exactly what you have been. That's why I'm surprised to hear you saying such nice things about fundamentalism.

Thomas: Fundamentalism? I thought we were discussing the resurrection.

Bertha: Oh!

Fesser: What is it, Bertha?

Bertha: I just realized something, I think. For the first time. Maybe the question of the resurrection is a separate question, and not just a piece of the fundamentalist agenda. I mean, you can't decide whether the resurrection really happened or not just

by taking polls of what people believe today and finding that
the same people who believe in the resurrection also believe in
the rest of the fundamentalist agenda—chauvinism and literalism and traditionalism and conservatism and militarism and
capitalism and a lot of other awful, oppressive things—and
finding out that the same people who believe that the resurrection didn't really happen also believe in equality and justice and
peace and compassion and ecology and . . .

Fesser: So what's your point, Bertha?

Bertha: That whatever combination of beliefs twentieth-century
fundamentalists concoct, that recipe can't be the real cause for
what happened two thousand years ago in Israel. I mean, causality can't work backwards, for one thing. And for another thing,
people's beliefs don't make a thing happen or not happen. The
thing either happened or it didn't, and you can't find that out by
taking Gallup polls of ideologies.

Fesser: Oh, of course. But surely there are relevant ideological
considerations which must be examined. The implications . . .

Bertha: You mean I'm wrong?

Fesser: No, no . . .

Bertha: Then I'm right.

Fesser: You're beginning to sound like Socrates.

Bertha: I'm beginning to wonder if that's so bad.

Solomon: May I ask a question, Professor?

Professor [surprised to hear from the silent one]: Certainly.

Solomon: Historians know of the tombs of saints and sages, don't
they? Saint Peter's tomb, and Muhammad's tomb, and so on?

Fesser: Yes.

Solomon: And those other tombs—they are all full, aren't they?

Fesser: Full?

Solomon: The saints and sages are all dead. Their bones are in
their tombs.

Fesser: Yes. The place is, anyway.

Solomon: And Jesus' tomb is there, in Jerusalem, isn't it?

Fesser: Yes.

Solomon: And it is empty.

Fesser [uncomfortable again]: Eh . . . yes . . .

Solomon: Where is the body?

Fesser: That was one of Socrates' questions.

Solomon: No, I mean I really want to know. Where is the body? What happened to the body?

Socrates: If I understand the New Testament correctly, it is here.

Fesser [scared, as if of a ghost]: What?

Socrates: The body of Christ is here. It's alive. He's risen.

Fesser: But he is supposed to have ascended back into heaven.

Socrates: In that body, yes. But he has another body, which is here on earth. At least the New Testament calls it that.

Fesser: Oh, you mean the church.

Socrates: Yes. But the way you say it, it seems you mean *"only* the church." In the New Testament, the church seems to be something much more than a human society that meets to remember a dead man and his teachings. It seems to be something more like a living organism, like the frog on the log rather than the bump on the log. Isn't that right? Have I understood your book correctly?

Ahmen: You have, Socrates.

Socrates: And a living organism has a living soul, a spirit. Did he not promise to send that Spirit? Perhaps that is the missing ingredient I sought for, the thing I saw in the New Testament but not here. Am I on the right track or not? Anyone?

Ahmen: You just hit the bull's eye, Socrates.

Fesser: Well, now, that is a matter of opinion and denominational differences, of course . . .

Ahmen: No, it isn't. It's a matter of what the New Testament says.

Fesser [holding it in]: Well . . . I am always glad to see a wide spectrum of opinions represented. I understand where you're coming from, Ahmen, I just don't happen to share your viewpoint.

Ahmen: I think you *don't* understand where I'm coming from,

Professor. Because it's not a *where*, it's a *who*.

Fesser [forced]: It's way past time to go. I wonder if Socrates is satisfied. Has your original question been answered, Socrates?

Socrates: More than answered. I began with the apparently innocuous question why you date your years around this man Jesus, and I was led by the inquiry into meeting him as something more than a man. Along the way I found the clear answer to my question—clear to me, at any rate.

Fesser: And what was the clear answer, Socrates?

Socrates: Years are divided by this man because he is the greatest thing that ever happened. Think of it! God becoming a man, dying, rising—why it's obviously the greatest thing imaginable, greater than *can* be imagined, perhaps. And that, I think, is why I believe it.

Thomas: What? You mean you believe it because it's crazy? *That's* crazy, especially for you, Socrates.

Socrates: No, I think it is rational. For it would take a spirit unimaginably greater and cleverer than yours or mine to invent such a story.

Thomas: Why?

Socrates: You admit the principle of causality, do you not? That the effect cannot be greater than the cause?

Thomas: Yes.

Socrates: And a myth is an effect of a myth-maker?

Thomas: Yes.

Socrates: Then the spiritual power of the myth cannot exceed the spiritual power of the myth-maker.

Thomas: That follows.

Socrates: If, then, Christianity is a myth, who is the myth-maker?

Thomas: I don't know.

Socrates: I know only One who could possibly have invented such a tremendous tale.

Thomas: You mean . . .

Socrates: Yes. I have been led by the tale back up to the Teller, who, I think, sent me here to learn of him through learning of his tale.

Bertha: Where do you go from here, Socrates?

Socrates: That's up to him. *[Bell for next class rings.]*

Bertha: No it isn't, Socrates. It's up to the third floor. There's the bell. We're late for our Comparative Religions class. *[Class laughs, leaves.]*

Fesser: Oh, don't forget, here's your reading list for next time. *[Passes it out at door.]* Please don't neglect academics in your enthusiasm. This is a university, after all . . .

Bertha [exiting with Socrates, whispering to him]: Sometimes I think a university is a morgue.

Socrates: Or a tomb.

Bertha: But the professor is a very wise man. Did you see the length of his reading lists?

Socrates: "They make broad their phylacteries . . . "

Bertha: What?

Socrates: Just quoting your Scriptures. I suppose I should not insult the academy. It was the invention of my favorite pupil, after all. But when it talks about a grape, I wonder why it has to squeeze out the juice and turn it into a prune.

Postscript from the *Boston Glob*

Boston Glob, Sept. 30, 1987: Police are investigating the mysterious disappearance of two men from the Broadener Library at Have It University yesterday: a transient known only as Flanagan, employed as a janitor at the library, and a student at Have It Divinity School registered under the name of Socrates. Police have found no clues as to the identity or the whereabouts of either.

According to Ms. Bertha Broadmind, a friend and fellow student of Socrates, the two missing persons suddenly disappeared from full view of herself and five other students at the Divinity School as the seven of them were together arguing in the library stacks.

The Rev. Bobbie Bub Battle, visiting from the Billie Bo Bible Basher School, where he teaches Southern Fried Apologetics, corroborated Ms. Broadmind's story. "The two of 'em jes' up an' left. Now I ain't 'sprized, mind you," Rev. Battle was quoted as saying, " 'Cuz this here place is the Divil's own home territory. I swan, they up an' git by devil-power."

Harry Tick, a graduate of Onion Theological Cemetery, doing postgraduate work at Have It, had a different explanation. "Mass delusion on a small scale," he insisted. "Freud explained it all long ago—and everything else, too." But Arthur Doxie, a graduate of Dullest Divinity School, disagreed. "It all depends on your hermeneutical, dispensational, eschatological, epistemological and sociopsychocultural assumptions," he said.

A fourth witness, Father I. Noitall, S.J., on leave from the Gregarious University in Levitican, insisted that the event seemed to fit the criteria for a genuine miracle, and said that he would initiate proceedings toward the eventual canonization of Socrates as a saint.

A fifth observer, moviemaker Steppen Wolfe, claimed to have filmed the event, but when the film was developed, the figure of Flanagan was wholly invisible. No explanation of this phenomenon was forthcoming.

All the witnesses agreed on the following details. At about 3 P.M., Broadmind, Battle, Tick, Doxie, Noitall and Wolfe were with Socrates in the stacks of the Broadener Library discussing some arcane theological subject which some said was the Trinity and others said was the divinity of Christ [Editor's Note: two primitive dogmas frequently appealed to by ultraconservatives]. The seven were interrupted by the sudden appearance of Flanagan, the janitor, who walked up to Socrates, ignoring the others, and said, "It's time to go now." When the others demanded to know who he was, he replied that he had different names in different ages, and mentioned a number among which were Raphael, Olorin and Gandalf.

As Flanagan touched Socrates, the two began to fade from the others' view. The last thing the observers heard was Socrates' question, "But why must I go now?" and Flanagan's answer,

"You're needed on the other side of the river." Some interpreted this saying symbolically, others literally. The literalists said
they expected Socrates to show up soon at Bussed-In College,
on the other side of the river from Have It.